Y0-BRX-114

Nakahara

Nakahara

Family Farming and Population in a
Japanese Village, 1717-1830

THOMAS C. SMITH

with Robert Y. Eng and Robert T. Lundy

STANFORD UNIVERSITY PRESS

Stanford, California   1977

WITHDRAWN

Rock Valley College
Educational Resources
Center

Stanford University Press
Stanford, California
© 1977 by the Board of Trustees of the
Leland Stanford Junior University
Printed in the United States of America
ISBN 0-8047-0928-9
LC 76-14273

B
652
34
56

To Old Friends Rachel and Zachary

Acknowledgments

In working on this book, I have accumulated many heavy debts of gratitude for friendly advice, criticism, and encouragement. Among those who read all or part of the manuscript and whose comments helped me in more ways than I can describe were Gary Allinson, Sei'ichi Ando, James Bartholomew, Harumi Befu, Woodrow Borah, Sidney Crawcour, Kingsley Davis, Ronald Dore, Peter Duus, Mark Fruin, Eugene Hammel, Akira Hayami, Chalmers Johnson, Byron Marshall, Helen and William McCullough, Irwin Scheiner, Jeanne M. Smith, Etienne van de Walle, Ann Waswo, James White, and Anthony Wrigley. In addition, I want to express my appreciation to Sei'ichi Ando, who helped greatly in getting the brush-written documents on which the book is based into more legible form, and to Akira Hayami, whose researches have been an important means of orienting my own efforts. The latter has given me much encouragement and at an early stage cleared the way of an extraordinary and unexpected obstacle. I hope that in some measure this book justifies his generosity.

Robert Eng, Robert Lundy, and Dana Morris made contributions as research assistants that I cannot properly thank them for now if I have not already done so, and I would be pleased to think they learned as much from our work together as I did. The work of Robert Eng and Robert Lundy, each on a separate chapter of the book, amounted to joint authorship of the chapters with me. I also wish to thank Ruth Iscol for her programming, and Hajimi Miyazaki for his patient collating of information from different population registers. A National Science Foundation grant made possible the bulk of the work and financed a summer's trip to Nakahara, and I received supplementary grants from the Institute of International Studies and the Center for Japanese and Korean Studies at the University of California, Berkeley. For all of this generous financial support I am deeply grateful.

T.C.S.

Contents

Tables and Figures

Nakahara

Chapter One Introduction

UNTIL RECENT years it was widely believed, if rarely stated, that the preindustrial economies of Western nations were very much like the economies of underdeveloped countries today. Writing in the 1930's, the English economic historian R. H. Tawney could conclude of China:

Insofar as the disorders of Chinese agriculture [have their source in defects of economic organization] . . . they are acute in degree but not unique in kind. They are one species of a genus which has been widely diffused, and which is characteristic, not of this nation or that, but of a particular phase of economic civilization. The persistence of an empirical technique based on venerable usage and impervious to science; the meagre output of foodstuffs which that technique produced; the waste of time and labour through the fragmentation of holdings; the absence of means of communication and the intolerable condition of such as existed; the narrow margin separating the mass of population from actual starvation and the periodical recurrence of local famines—such phenomena, if exception be made of a few favoured regions, were until recently the commonplaces of Western economic life.[1]

But doubts regarding this straightforward view began to grow after World War II, as social scientists came to contend with the problems of economic development in backward countries. What had at first appeared to be a cultural obstacle, expressed as an almost capricious insistence on irrational, self-defeating behavior, was seen increasingly as a shrewd economic adjustment to the cir-

[1] Numeral superscripts refer to the Notes, pp. 165–73, primarily for citations of sources and relevant collateral material. Footnotes are designated by superscript letters.

cumstance of poverty. As the attention of economists accordingly shifted from cultural to objective constraints, the suspicion grew that these constraints were not, in fact, closely similar to those faced earlier by the industrializing West. This idea was dramatically confirmed by Simon Kuznets's persuasive estimate in 1954 that on the eve of industrialization most countries of Western Europe already had per capita incomes several times higher than those of underdeveloped countries today.[a]

Western countries, then, appear to have been rich, by global standards, even before the miracle of modern industry appeared. And that miracle may have been as much a result of wealth as a new source of it. Instead of asking, "How did poor Western countries industrialize?" we ought perhaps to ask, "How did poor Western countries become rich enough to industrialize?" The answer would not seem to be the obvious one: that Western economies expanded output in an unparalleled way before industrializing. Other parts of the world have enjoyed great periods of expansion. China, for instance, almost certainly stood for many centuries on a higher technological and organizational level than Europe. Yet something must have gone "wrong" in this case. Somehow gains in output were not translated into long-term gains in per capita income as they were in the West.

Population growth may have been a decisive influence in this respect. Population in the West lagged or was restrained behind the slow growth of output for centuries; otherwise, per capita income could not have reached the levels it did. In China, where expansion of output over long periods was surely massive, population cannot

[a] Kuznets selected eight advanced countries—the United States, the United Kingdom, Canada, France, Germany, Sweden, Denmark, and Italy—for which records of national income for the last three-quarters of a century were available. Then, using the growth rates per decade in per capita income expressed in constant prices, he extrapolated back from present levels to derive an approximation of the per capita income of each country at the time when 60 percent or more of its labor force was employed in agriculture. These derived figures were then compared with the 1953 per capita incomes of underdeveloped countries. Kuznets, "Underdeveloped Countries and the Preindustrial Phase of Advanced Countries," pp. 142–45.

have lagged to the same extent as in Europe. The lag must have been less marked, or more ephemeral, or more nearly canceled out by subsequent periods of rapid growth. The immediate demographic reason for this is not clear, but it would not be surprising to find that Chinese fertility was higher than European for long periods.

In any case, we know that European fertility was relatively low. Western Europe showed a pattern of late female marriage (and a high proportion of women never marrying at all) that seems never to have occurred anywhere else in the world. Elsewhere, the rule for women is and presumably has been early and nearly universal marriage.[b] Nor is the European pattern a recent development—a result, perhaps, of changing employment patterns, democratic ideology, or the gradual liberation of women. On the contrary, it was even more marked in the eighteenth century, when the mean age of first marriage for women was about 25 and the proportion of women never married at age 50 was about 15 percent. How far back this pattern goes is uncertain, but the bulk of the evidence suggests that it came into existence over most of Western Europe in the sixteenth and seventeenth centuries.[2]

Late marriage and a high proportion of persons never marrying were unquestionably powerful restraints on fertility. Marriage at 25 or 26 instead of at 17 or 18 reduced by about half the number of children European women could bear during married life, and this, together with the high ratio of celibate women, resulted in crude annual birth rates for the eighteenth century that were usually little more than 30 per 1,000 population, as compared to rates in the 40's and 50's in underdeveloped countries today.[3] Moreover, these low rates were not significantly affected by either contraception or low natural fertility. During equal intervals of marriage at equal

[b] The proportion of unmarried women aged 20–24 in Asian and Middle Eastern countries at various dates between 1920 and 1952 went as low as 2 percent (Korea, 1930) and as high as 31 percent (Japan, 1920), but was generally between 15 and 25 percent. This compares with percentages ranging between 60 and 86 percent for Western European countries in 1900. See Hajnal, "European Marriage Patterns in Perspective," especially pp. 102–4.

ages, European women in the eighteenth century typically bore not fewer but more children, by a substantial margin, than women in underdeveloped countries do.[c]

Thus restrictions on marriage were critical in restraining European population growth even as output expanded. The resulting rise in per capita income tended to expand the consumption of goods produced by secondary and tertiary industry, increase the division of labor, encourage the development of more complex and specialized commercial and financial institutions, and call forth more innovative entrepreneurs, more saving, and more investment. Lower fertility had other advantages as well. It kept the ratio of workers (ages 15–65) to total population relatively high—perhaps around 60 percent, as compared to 50 or 55 percent in many developing countries today.[4] Moreover, much less in the way of new capital was required annually to provide goods and services for additional population. For all these reasons, a restricted population may have been an essential precondition of industrialization.

For the hypothesis that low population growth over a protracted period was essential to subsequent industrialization, Japan is a strategic case. Here, in the eighteenth century, we have a country geographically and culturally remote from Europe, cut off from the benefits of worldwide trade, with a technology and a population density (relative to arable land) similar to China's; yet today it is one of the world's most technically advanced nations, having begun industrialization as long ago as the late nineteenth century and gained momentum over two generations with little deliberate help from the West. Did or did not Japan also experience an extended rise in per capita income prior to industrialization? It can be argued that such a rise occurred. Between the beginning of the Tokugawa regime in 1600 and the Meiji Restoration of the mid-nineteenth

[c]For example, age-specific marital fertility in Sweden in 1871–80, the rates of which were about the same as in European parishes in the eighteenth century, was higher in every age group than that for India in 1961–63. For the 15–19 group the Swedish rate was 2.5 times the Indian; this declined to a 30-percent advantage for ages 25–34, but rose from that point to an 80-percent advantage for Swedish women aged 40–44. See Kumar, "A Comparison between Current Indian Fertility and Late Nineteenth-Century Swedish and Finnish Fertility," p. 271.

century, Japanese output unquestionably expanded greatly, though the precise timing of the expansion is uncertain; and during the latter half of this period, from 1721 at the latest, the national population was nearly static.

There is much about this seeming parallel in rising per capita income that is doubtful. Nothing is more doubtful—or more critical—than the mechanism of population restraint in Japan, and little is known of that. If population was held in check by deliberate controls over fertility, we should have in some respects a functional equivalent of the European marriage pattern. But if population was checked mainly by famine, as some historians believe, we should have reason to doubt the economic expansion and consequent rise in per capita income after 1721. In this book we seek to add to an understanding of these problems in the only way presently possible: by detailed analysis of the dynamics of a small local population. First, though, something must be said about Tokugawa population generally.

The size of the population of Japan in 1600, when the Tokugawa victory inaugurated an era of peace, security, and orderly government after many years of civil war, is uncertain. Estimates range from under 10 million to over 18 million.[5] There is general agreement, nevertheless, that the population grew substantially between then and 1721, when the commoner population was counted for the first time and found to number 26 million. Scattered local records confirm an increase; so do the remarkable growth in towns and the impressive expansion of cultivated land in the seventeenth century.[6]

But it is not really until the eighteenth century that we get onto something like firm demographic ground. Earlier, the Tokugawa government had required every town and village to compile a register of inhabitants at regular intervals (annually in most places), and in 1721, these local jurisdictions were ordered to report their currently registered populations up the administrative hierarchy to the Shogunal government in Edo, where the figures were aggregated by province for the entire country. This administrative census (as we shall call it) was repeated in 1726, and thereafter at six-year intervals until 1846, when the system lapsed. National totals survive for 18 of these censuses, and provincial totals for 10.[7]

In view of their early dates, it is hardly surprising that these censuses leave something to be desired. *Samurai* and some smaller groups were entirely outside the registration system and consequently were not reported. Infants were usually not listed until the first annual registration after birth; hence many died unrecorded. The form and standards of registration were not uniform from one region to another, and some Japanese scholars believe that inadvertent omissions may have increased over time as a result of internal migration.[8]

Nonetheless, there is general agreement that these early census data reflect population *trends* rather accurately.[9] This qualified confidence is based partly on the study of local registers in long chronological series, in which one can follow individuals from birth to death, note persons who enter or leave the register without explanation, and check the comprehensiveness and consistency of registration in many ways. This kind of scrutiny reveals numerous recording errors and scattered periods of either near-perfect or extremely lax recording; but there is no obvious, systematic bias in the registration of commoners, excepting the late registration of infants.

At the provincial and national levels, population totals change plausibly from one census to another; known famines and epidemics are clearly reflected; unaccountable or unbelievable changes are rare.[10] Other signs are also reassuring: population trends within regions tend to be consistent across important administrative boundaries;[d] districts with a gradual expansion of cultivated land generally show long-term population increases as well;[11] and mountain areas lose population to plains, basins, and

---

[d]This can be seen from the provincial data in Sekiyama, *Kinsei Nihon no jinko kōzō*, pp. 137 *et seq*. For example, all five provinces of the Kinai, which were fragmented into many fiefs, suffered population declines between 1721 and 1846; and the Hiroshima and Chōshū fiefs, which were both large and were neighbors in southwestern Honshu, registered exceptionally large gains.

polder (a tendency that was noted by contemporary writers and corresponds to patterns of commercial and industrial development).[12]

If the census data may be taken as reliable indicators of the overall trend, it is clear that there was no growth of the national population between 1721 and 1846. Taking 1721 as 100, the index of population fluctuated between 96 and 104, and stood at 103 in 1846. Over the entire period the average annual increase was 0.03 percent, a rate that would require more than two millennia to double the population.[e] Regionally, as might be expected, the picture was varied. Population declined in the northeast and in central Japan but increased along the Japan Sea and in the southwest. However, both growth and decline were remarkably modest. Only 11 of 69 provinces had an average annual increase of more than 0.2 percent over the whole period; one of these, Hokkaido, was a newly settled area of fast growth, and four others were small islands (see Table 1.1). Declines were even more limited, with only one province suffering a decline of more than 0.2 percent.

Even these figures may exaggerate the amount of change, since the fastest-growing provinces had minuscule populations. When regions rather than provinces are taken as the unit, the range of variation is significantly narrowed (Table 1.2). This is not to say that regional differences were not significant, or to deny that much can be learned from them; but their importance should not be exaggerated.

A few comparisons with other preindustrial populations will put these rates in perspective. The population of China is thought to have approximately doubled between 1749 and 1819, growing by about 1 percent each year.[13] In the Scandinavian countries, annual growth in the second half of the eighteenth century was 0.5 percent

[e] The reader may compare this rate for 1721–1846 with the rate of 0.16 percent given by Hanley and Yamamura for the period 1721–1872. He should be cautioned, however, that the registration of 1872 by the Meiji government included a large population not reflected in the Tokugawa figures. The most important new registrants were the *samurai*, who numbered about two million in the 1872 registration even though many former samurai were registered as commoners. Sekiyama, pp. 310–11; Hanley and Yamamura, "Population Trends," p. 492.

TABLE I.I

Average Annual Provincial Population Growth Rates,
1721–1846

Growth rate (percent)	Number of provinces	Growth rate (percent)	Number of provinces
negative	25	0.21–0.30	7
0.00–0.10	12	0.31–0.40	3
0.11–0.20	21	over 0.40	1*

SOURCE: Sekiyama, *Kinsei Niho no jinkō kōzō*, p. 137.
  * Hokkaido.

TABLE I.2

Average Annual Rates of Population Change by Region,
1721–1846

Region	Rate of change	Region	Rate of change
Kinki	−0.05	Hokuriku	0.13
Tōkai	0.05	San'in	0.18
Kantō	−0.11	San'yō	0.15
Tōhoku	−0.10	Shikoku	0.20
Tōsan	0.08	Kyūshū	0.10

for Sweden, 1.2 percent for Finland, 0.3 percent for Denmark, and 0.7 percent for Norway.[14] Most of the countries of Western Europe recorded annual increases ranging from 0.5 percent to 1.0 percent during 1801–50 (a period in most cases prior to industrialization).[15] It is likely that the Japanese population itself grew at a rate approaching 1.0 percent in the century before 1700. All these figures are weighted national averages of regional highs and lows; yet nearly all are very much higher than the rate of even the fastest-growing regions in eighteenth-century Japan.

The rapid growth of Japanese population in the seventeenth century, followed by virtual stagnation from about 1700 to 1867, is a phenomenon that has long been of great diagnostic interest to historians; and until recently they were nearly unanimous in explaining it in Malthusian terms. The Tokugawa conquest, they argued, released powerful expansionist forces in the economy, and population grew as output expanded. But the technical and institutional limits of economic expansion were reached in the early eighteenth century.[16] Population began to press against food supply, and repeatedly crept up only to be thrown back to the old levels by large-scale famines and epidemics. For over a century the commoner population fluctuated around 26 million; and this ceiling, it is pointed out, was not broken through until the Meiji period, when the economy began to grow again under the influence of political change, international trade, and technological borrowing.

Irene Taeuber expressed the general opinion in 1958:

The course of population growth in Tokugawa Japan tended toward the creation of numbers that were excessive in relation to levels of production and income. In fact, such an increase of population as would reduce per capita income, lessen vitality, and increase mortality was a natural correlate of the economy, the system of government, and the social structure of the Bakufu government.[17]

In support of this view, it could be pointed out that little new land was brought under cultivation between 1721 and 1846; that large towns ceased to grow in the first half of the eighteenth century, many actually losing population; that the great Kyōhō and Temmei famines of the eighteenth century were on an unprecedented scale;[f] and that flights from the land and peasant uprisings increased markedly after 1700. In the light of such evidence, so transparent did the economic origins of demographic change seem to historians that they often cited the stagnation of Japanese population as positive proof that the economy had ceased to grow around 1700.[18]

However, two developments of the last fifteen years have called this view of Tokugawa history into question. One is the accumulation of empirical (and often quantitative) local studies by young Japanese economic historians, whose findings on the whole suggest not a stagnant but a growing economy in the eighteenth century.[19]

Apparently, crop yields were increasing through improved va-

[f]Surveying data from a number of scattered villages, Hanley stresses that mortality in Tokugawa Japan was comparable to that in Europe prior to 1850 and "not unlike that of Japan in the early twentieth century" ("Fertility, Mortality, and Life Expectancy," p. 141).

rieties and more intensive fertilization. Over much of the country rural trade and industry were growing. Nearly all branches of industry benefited from important technical innovations. Transport improved, and guild restrictions on the production and sale of goods were broken through. The consumption of manufactured goods among the peasantry increased. The number of schools catering to commoners grew enormously. And so on.

The second new development has been the adaptation to Japanese records of the methods perfected by Louis Henry for the demographic exploitation of French parish registers.[20] Using Henry's approach, one can calculate for the Tokugawa period a large number of precise measures, such as age-specific mortality and fertility, expectation of life, nuptiality, and the spacing of births. Only a few studies using these methods have been completed in Japan to date.[g] All concern small rural populations scattered on the Pacific side of Honshu roughly between Okayama on the south and Lake Suwa on the north—economically the most advanced part of the country and an area that showed relatively little change in population in the eighteenth century. Even this region is sparsely represented, however; other regions, and towns everywhere, remain nearly untouched.[21]

Clearly, these isolated data—representing a handful of villages out of tens of thousands—do not allow us to generalize about the movement of Tokugawa population as a whole. But it is striking that none of them reveal the high rates of mortality and fertility implied by the Malthusian interpretation; on the contrary, rates are moderate or even low by preindustrial standards. This is true even after the rates are adjusted upward, as they must be, to take account of infant births and deaths obscured by the system of delayed registration (see pp. 54–55). As will be seen in later chapters, the ad-

---

[g]Published studies using age-specific rates, for instance, are almost wholly the work of Hayami Akira (and his collaborators), Sasaki Yōichirō, and Susan Hanley. The overall scarcity of work derived from Henry's techniques exists because the major effort so far has been collecting and processing data, in addition to devising a strategy for computer analysis. This time-consuming but essential spadework, chiefly conducted by Professors Hayami and Sasaki, has now reached the stage at which we can soon expect a great increase in published results.

justed rates are as low as or lower than the corresponding rates for most eighteenth-century European parishes for which we have estimates. Let us put aside for the time being the question of mortality, where the estimates are less reliable than they might be, and consider only fertility, where we can be more confident about the low level and can also say something about probable causes.

In the first place, it is clear that fertility was not low on account of restrictions on marriage comparable to those in Europe. The mean age of first marriage for females was well below the European level, though considerably above that in many underdeveloped countries today; and almost all women seem to have married. The decisive fact, however, is that age-specific marital fertility was distinctly lower in the few Tokugawa villages so far studied than in most European counterparts. During equal intervals at equal ages, married women in these villages had fewer children than did married women in Europe (see p. 60).

It seems unlikely that Japanese women were relatively less fertile in any biological sense; one would expect a physical handicap like this to show up in higher mortality, but the level of female mortality in these same villages was much like that in Europe.[h] Suckling practices and sexual taboos can powerfully affect the level of natural fertility of a population, the one by prolonging the sterile period after childbirth, and the other by restricting the frequency of intercourse. But to our knowledge nothing is known about either subject as far as the Tokugawa period is concerned. On the other hand, we learn from literary and legal sources that abortion and infanticide were widely practiced in the Tokugawa period, apparently by all classes and conditions of people.[22] And Professor Hayami Akira has adduced strong circumstantial evidence tending to show that some form of limitation on births was practiced in Yokouchi, one of

[h] "The recent findings that the onset and maintenance of regular menstrual function in the human female are each dependent on the maintenance of a minimum weight for height . . . imply that undernutrition and energy-requiring activities may affect the fecundity of marginally nourished populations far more than has been realized heretofore." Frisch, "Demographic Implications of Biological Determinants of Female Fecundity," p. 1.

TABLE 1.3

Crude Birth and Death Rates in Yokouchi, 1671–1871

(Unadjusted for late registration)

Period	Birth rate per 1,000	Death rate per 1,000	Natural increase per 1,000
1671–1700	35.3	25.5	9.8
1701–25	39.8	25.5	14.3
1726–50	28.8	21.0	7.8
1751–75	26.3	16.4	9.9
1776–1800	20.1	19.4	0.7
1801–25	23.5	19.6	3.9
1826–50	21.4	18.3	3.1
1851–71	23.7	18.4	5.3
1671–1775	32.5	22.1	10.4
1776–1871	22.2	18.9	3.3
1671–1871	27.3	20.5	6.8

SOURCE: Data from Hayami, *Kinsei nōson*, p. 160. Averages for 1671–1775 and 1776–1871 are my calculations from Hayami's data.

several Tokugawa villages of which, thanks to him, we have detailed knowledge.

Hayami's study of Yokouchi is based on a series of annual population registers running from 1671 to 1871, with 53 missing years.
During roughly the first century of this period the population of the
village grew steadily and fairly rapidly; from 1776 to 1871 population was nearly constant. Thus Yokouchi approximates, with a time
lag, the demographic experience of the nation: secular growth followed by secular stagnation. This transition, in Yokouchi, was accompanied by a sharp decline in fertility and no rise in mortality
(see Table 1.3). The crude birth rate fell from 32 percent during the
first century to 22 percent during the second—almost one-third—
and the crude death rate, instead of rising, fell slightly.

The leveling out of population growth in Yokouchi was undoubtedly due largely to this extraordinary fall in fertility, though there
was also some net loss of population through migration after
1775.[23] We can also detect lessened fertility by comparing the age-
specific marital fertility of women born before 1700 with that of

women born in the period 1751–1800. In every five-year age group the earlier cohort had more children; and the average number of children born to a woman married from age 20 through 49 was 5.5 in the first cohort, and 3.2 in the second—a ratio of 1.8 to 1.[24] In this case, certainly, we can rule out a change in suckling practices or sexual taboos as an explanation, since the drop in fertility is so sharp. It is also difficult to believe that fecundity could have declined that fast. Hayami is probably correct, therefore, in attributing the fertility decline to some form of family limitation.[25]

This very incomplete sketch of present knowledge of Tokugawa population is enough to suggest, at least, that the powerful population growth of the seventeenth century may have been checked after 1721 not by a rise in deaths but by a voluntary limitation on marital fertility. Clearly, a great many more local studies will be needed before this or any other hypothesis can carry any great weight, and judging from the history of such studies in France, we are in for many surprises—and revisions—along the way. The overall picture is almost certainly more complex than we can possibly imagine now. Local populations are not miniatures of national populations, like them in everything but size, but fragments of a gigantic mosaic, in which each additional piece, at an early stage of research, may put the whole in new perspective.

It was this possibility, as well as the desire to learn something about demographic history, that prompted us some years ago to begin the study of the population registers and land records of the village we call Nakahara. Although the choice of Nakahara was almost wholly adventitious, determined by the accessibility of the materials, the village proved an interesting one. It was not located outside the geographical region of previous studies, as one would have wished; but the land registers turned out to be more reliable than initially expected, permitting us to touch on matters often beyond the reach of village studies of population, and various challenging points emerged.

Vital rates in Nakahara were similar to those found by Hayami in Yokouchi. Fertility, though remarkably low by comparison with eighteenth-century European parishes, was somewhat above mortality (again reinforcing doubts of the traditional view that Tokugawa population was held in check after 1721 by high mortality). Nuptiality made only a marginal contribution to low fertility. Marriage for females was young and nearly universal, though widowhood (as a result of women marrying considerably younger than men) and divorce were both common, and remarriage was less frequent than we had imagined.

Although the major check on fertility was clearly within marriage, as levels of age-specific marital fertility confirmed, the tests devised by Henry for family limitation did not yield a positive result. In time, we perceived that the population was practicing sex-selective infanticide, a form of family limitation not detectable under certain circumstances by the tests just mentioned; and there was a tendency to use this practice to balance the sexes of the sibling set at each birth order after the second. This suggested that infanticide was not wholly a function either of poverty or of momentary desperation but in part a method of planning the sex composition and ultimate size of the family. The explanation of this behavior, if found outside Nakahara (as it must be before being accepted as historically significant), may lie in the fiercely competitive nature of farming as reflected in the land registers, and in the relation of family size and composition to farm size and farming efficiency.

Before turning to the evidence on these and other points, however, we must briefly examine the character and reliability of Nakahara's records.

Chapter Two   The Sources

JAPANESE HISTORICAL demography has not yet evolved a set of generally recognized procedures for dealing with the many special problems raised by Tokugawa population registers. Since procedure cannot be exhaustively described in each set of published results it is often impossible for the reader to know precisely what methods were used, even at critical points. For this reason, and because of the unfamiliarity of most Western readers with Tokugawa population registers, it seems essential to begin with a general description of these documents and the methods adopted to cope with their most troublesome features. Our objective is not to tell everything, but to give the reader a reasonable idea of what has been done, so that he can make some judgment of the reliability and possible uses of the results.

Types of Population Register

The term "population register," which we use generically to refer to all village registers containing demographic information, has no actual Tokugawa equivalent, since Tokugawa administrators referred to these registers by specific name only. There were three types of population register in Nakahara, each of them compiled annually in the sixth lunar month.[1] In order of importance, both for us and for contemporaries, they were the *shūmon aratamechō*, the *zōgenchō*, and the *hōkōninchō*.[a]

---

[a] We use the shortened terms here for convenience. In archival listings each register is usually identified by the full wording and date, appended to the name of the village (*mura*) in question. Using our pseudonym "Nakahara," the full titles would

The *shūmon aratamechō* (or *SAC*) was the basic register of village population. Ideally, it listed everyone living in the village on the day it was compiled except infants born after New Year's Day (an important and awkward exception to which we shall return). Individuals were listed by household, and households appear in a nearly unvarying order in successive years. Within each household the householder was always listed first, followed by other members roughly in order of nearness of their relationship to him (or occasionally her), taking sex and age into account.

For each person the usual items entered were name, age, sex, and relationship to householder. Wives (and sometimes widows) were usually entered without a name, being listed merely as "wife" immediately following the husband's name, or as "so-and-so's wife" if other entries intervened. Thus the household of Nakahara's village priest had the following entries in 1729 and 1730:

1729, 6TH MONTH

Ryōsetsu, 26; male; householder
Grandmother, 76; female; grandmother
   [Note]: died 9th month
Wife, 23; female; spouse [of Ryōsetsu]
Fumi, 5; female; daughter

1730, 6TH MONTH

Ryōsetsu, 27; male; householder
Wife, 24; female; spouse
Fumi, 6; female; daughter

Everyone, including servants, was listed as a member of one or another household; we never find unattached individuals. Single-person households were not uncommon, but the one person was invariably designated "householder," making it clear that he or she constituted a distinct household for purposes of registration.

---

be: (1) *Nakahara mura shūmon oaratamechō*; (2) *Nakahara mura zōnin genin oaratamechō*; (3) *Nakahara mura sho hōkōnin oaratamechō*. These registers, along with much other manuscript material from "Nakahara," are housed in the archives of Meiji University in Tokyo. In using them we were greatly aided by the assistance of Mr. Kanzaki and Miss Kukida of that institution.

Whether all such households were separate residential units is uncertain, but in most cases they probably were. The single member, usually the last survivor of a larger household, was simply one stage in a family cycle, which would end with the demise of the household through death or migration, or perhaps with its expansion through marriage or adoption.

Villagers who were presently living and working elsewhere were listed as members of their households, with a note on current residence (and often employer's identity). If such people stayed away too long, however, they were apt to be dropped from the registers, normally with an indication of why but sometimes without explanation. In the latter case, we cannot distinguish permanent migration from death as the cause of departure.

How the *SAC* was actually compiled is uncertain. By law, the village headman was required to go from house to house on registration day, or at least consult each househead separately;[2] and each househead in fact affixed his seal beneath his name in the register to confirm the entries for his house. But this procedure may sometimes have been short-cut. For example, mistakes concerning ages, once in the record, were often perpetuated for years on end, suggesting that one year's register was sometimes made up, at least in part, by copying the previous year's register with suitable changes. But this does not imply that the legally prescribed procedure was omitted: the registrar may have consulted househeads on the membership of households but relied mainly on the previous year's register for ages (where memory was most likely to be faulty).

After the *SAC* for a given year was compiled, changes that occurred before the next registration through births, deaths, migration, marriage, or adoption were sometimes noted in the margins or between lines, presumably at the time of occurrence. More often, corrections were entered on narrow slips of tissue paper called *harigami*, which were pasted in at the top edge and could be lifted to consult entries underneath. We call all entries that were made after the annual registration "emendations," whether they appear on *harigami* or otherwise.

Emendations always indicated the identity of the person involved and the nature of the event, often in considerable detail. For example, when a girl married out of the village—and about 80 percent of them did—the emendation usually recorded the name of the groom, his househead's name, and the province, district, fief, and village where he lived. Taken together, the emendations would provide an excellent system of vital registration, except that many *harigami* have been lost and that a high proportion of these and other emendations do not record the day or month of an event, especially after 1750. Even when an emendation has been lost, however, we rarely lose the event itself, which can usually be recovered from one of the other registers or inferred from a subsequent *SAC*.

The *zōgenchō* (ZGC) was the annual vital register and record of migratory movement. Each person entering or leaving the village, for whatever reason, was fully identified by name, age, sex, name of househead, and relationship to him; and the reason for the entry or departure was recorded. The purpose of compiling the *ZGC*, which contained no information not found in the *SAC*, was obviously convenience: one could tell at a glance who had left and entered the village during the year without searching through the bulky *SAC*. To us, the *ZGC* is useful mainly as a supplement to the *SAC* when entries in the latter are illegible or emendations are missing; and one can often reconstruct the village population from it in years when the entire *SAC* has been lost.

The *hōkōninchō* (HC) was a register of servants (*hōkōnin*), both those from Nakahara who lived and worked elsewhere and those from other villages who lived and worked in Nakahara. Like the *ZGC*, it can be used to supplement or check the *SAC*. Its greatest value is when—through some lapse of the registrar or the loss of both *SAC* and *ZGC*—a person suddenly disappears from the record. It can then be determined from the *HC* whether he was working outside the village or had left for some other reason.

Japanese Ages

The traditional Japanese system of counting age, in use throughout our period, reckons a child as age 1 at birth and adds an additional year on each New Year's Day thereafter. Consequently, a child born on the last day of the year will be age 1 on that day and age 2 on the next, whereas a child born the day after New Year's would not attain age 2 until the following New Year's, 364 days later. This would cause no difficulty in calculating the exact age of those born in Nakahara if the date as well as the fact of birth had been regularly entered. But a high proportion of emendations on *harigami* are missing; and those we have, though presumably made at the time of birth, were dated by month only in some periods.

In our calculations, then, we must usually depend on the first *annual* registration of a child in the *SAC*, together with the record of the birth (always undated) in the *ZGC*. However, neither *SAC* nor *ZGC* registered children until after their first New Year's, so that they were always entered as two years old when first registered; and all we usually know about a birth date is that it was prior to the New Year's preceding registration and after the New Year's before that. In Nakahara both documents were compiled during the sixth month; thus the actual age of children at registration was between six and eighteen lunar months (see Figure 2.1). We have consequently treated all children in the record as exactly one year old at first registration—that is, we have assumed that births were randomly distributed over the preceding year.

We have also corrected all ages in the registers to standard Western ages by subtracting one full year from the registered age. It should be remembered that this represents age in the sixth month of a given year; therefore, a person's Western age at some event during the year, such as marriage or death, must be calculated from this base—a problem discussed in the next section. The point to be noted here is that all ages cited in this book are standard Western ages computed in this way, unless Japanese ages are specifically indicated by placing JA before the age (as when we say a child is registered for the first time at JA 2).

Dating Events

How are we to determine a person's age at marriage, death, migration, and so on, since these events were usually recorded without day or month? Here we must distinguish "gap" years, when the

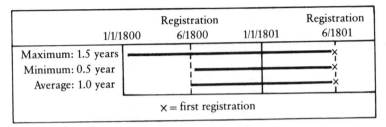

Fig. 2.1. Possible ages of Nakahara children at first registration (JA 2)

SAC and *ZGC* are both missing, from years in which the *SAC* series is unbroken. With an intact series it is simple to identify the year of an event, since one year's *SAC* will not reflect it and the next one will; and often an emendation to the first *SAC* also tells us that the event occurred after the register was compiled. But we cannot normally date the event precisely during the year.

We have therefore dated all events except birth exactly midway between the two *SAC* that surround them. For convenience we take the midway point to be the first day of the year of the second *SAC*. Thus the date midway between the registration of 1750 and 1751 would be 1/1/1751—New Year's Day. The age of the person at a given event, therefore, is his or her age in the second register minus 0.5 year (or that in the first register plus 0.5 year). For example, a woman who was 30 in the 1750 *SAC* and died between that registration and the next is counted as dying at age 30.5.

Births are an exception to the rule for dating. This is because on the average they occur, as already explained, one full year prior to the first registration of the child at JA 2. Consequently, in calculating the parent's age at the birth of a child, we subtract 1.0 years rather than 0.5 from age at the time of the birth's registration. If the mother is JA 30 at the time, for example, we would first subtract one year to convert her age to standard age, and then another full year to calculate her age at the time of the actual birth—in this case 28.

Error in Dating Events

We have assumed that events of all kinds were distributed randomly during the year, and therefore that the midpoint in any twelve-month period will represent the median of occurrences in that interval. Since demographic events, in reality, always follow seasonal rhythms, this assumption entails some error; the question is how much. We can estimate the divergence by examining events that are month-dated in emendations often enough to give a sample of reasonable size. Three kinds of events offer usable samples: births, deaths, and marriages into Nakahara from the outside.

For each type of event we assign each individual occurrence a number corresponding to the lunar month in which it took place; 1 for the first month, 2 for the second, and so on. Then we sum the numbers and divide by the number of occurrences. If occurrences were distributed randomly and our sample were sufficiently large, the quotient should be 6.5; any variance from this will reflect either a sampling error or some actual seasonality of distribution and a corresponding error in our dating system. The results of this test are:

	Births	Deaths	Marriages in
Sample	147	110	35
Quotient	7.5	6.1	5.1
Dating error in months	+1.0	−0.4	−1.4

Thus our dating assumption appears not to entail an error of more than 1.5 months, or 12.5 percent; and it is only 3.3 percent in the case of mortality.

Registration Year

In later chapters when we refer to demographic events during a particular year (e.g. deaths during the year 1800), we mean not the calendar year but the registration year: that is, the twelve lunar months (in some years thirteen) between successive *SAC* registrations in the sixth month. Thus the registration year is similar to a fiscal year in modern business and governmental organizations, with one important difference. The fiscal year is designated by the year in which it begins: for example, July 1974 to July 1975 is fiscal year 1974 (or 1974–75). For reasons of accounting convenience, the registration year in Nakahara was designated by the year in which it ended: thus 6/1800 to 6/1801 is registration year 1801. All nondemographic events, of course, are referred to by calendar year;

and no correction is made in either calendar or registration years from the lunar to the modern calendar.

Infant Mortality

As already explained, children were registered as "births" at the first registration after their first New Year's, and actual ages at registration ranged from six to eighteen months. Consequently, many children died before registration and never come under our observation. For lack of a better term, we refer to this group as "unregistered infants."

The omission of unregistered infants is the most serious defect of the *SAC* in Nakahara and in all other Tokugawa villages, and to some extent it distorts nearly all demographic measures. It lowers all birth and death rates below their actual levels, lengthens the mean interval between (registered) births, reduces the mean age of mothers at the birth of the last (registered) child, and diminishes the mean size of (registered) completed families. In Nakahara these distortions probably do not interfere much with comparisons between one generation and another, or even one social group and another, since mortality after standard age 1 differs relatively little from one 25-year period to another or between distinguishable social strata.

However, unless adjustments are made for unregistered infants, the loss of their births and deaths from the data vitiates the comparison of rates with European parishes, where the problem of late registration is at a minimum. It even makes comparisons between Tokugawa villages somewhat risky, since these differ not only in the infant death rate but also in the time lived before registration. Suppose, for example, that a village compiled its *SAC* on the first day of the calendar year rather than in the sixth month. Instead of ranging from six to eighteen months, the age of children at first registration would then vary from less than one day to a maximum of twelve months. Even if the actual mortality curves in Nakahara and in this village were identical in every respect, therefore, the proportion of children dying before registration would clearly be different, since the mean age at registration would be twelve months in one case and six months in the other.

Cause-Unknown Entries

Allied in principle to the question just discussed, though arising from a different cause, is the problem of twelve children who entered the Nakahara record at JA 2 but were classified as "cause-unknown entries" rather than births. We did this because shortly after entry they underwent jumps of one to several years in recorded age, raising the possibility that the initial JA 2 notation had been mistaken, and that the children were in fact late registrations. If so, they may have been born in the village and registered late through negligence; or, in view of the ambiguous circumstances surrounding their entry, they may have been adopted from outside Nakahara without the fact being noted. If they were adopted, their classification as "cause unknown" is innocuous from the viewpoint of fertility. But if they were in fact natural children of the registered parents, by using this classification we should have missed twelve births (and underestimated fertility in Nakahara by 2 percent).

Gap Years

One of the most troublesome problems in using Tokugawa population registers is that occasional gaps occur in almost all chronological series of these documents; and Nakahara is no exception (see Table 2.1). Where a gap occurs in the SAC but is bridged by the ZGC (exits and entries), the population during the gap can be fully reconstructed. But where both records are missing, only some of the exits and entries can be reconstructed from later registers.

Consider first the case of exits. A person who has been in the population all along and exits during a gap will be found to have departed when the record resumes. The question is not whether he exited, but when and why. For all practical purposes, the time of exit can be assigned satisfactorily either by placing the exit midway in the period during which an unobserved exit was possible or by fixing a month and year in this period by random number.[b]

---

[b] We used the random method, but would not do so again; the other is simpler and probably as accurate.

TABLE 2.1
Missing Years in Nakahara Population Registers

SAC lost	ZGC lost	HC lost	Both SAC and ZGC lost
1721	1717–18	1718	1721
1728	1721	1721	1736–38
1731	1724	1726–27	1744
1736–38	1726	1738	1749
1741	1736–38	1744	1752
1743–45	1744	1752	1777
1749	1746	1756	1782–84
1752–59	1749	1758	1787
1762–63	1752	1770	1801
1765	1768	1774–76	
1771–74	1770	1789–91	All three registers lost
1776–77	1775	1793	
1781–90	1777	1801	1721
1797–1801	1782–84	1808	1738
1804	1787	1812	1744
1809–11	1792–93	1814–16	1752
1820	1801	1818–20	1801
1822	1812	1822	
1824–25	1816	1824–25	
	1818	1827–28	
	1829–30		

Assigning the reason for an unobserved exit is obviously more difficult, since we have less to go on and the issue is more consequential. Did the person die or did he migrate? In order not to underestimate mortality, we used a somewhat arbitrary procedure. All persons exiting unobserved whose last registered age was over 49 or under 6 were automatically classified as deaths; this has a certain justification, in that most observed exits beyond these age limits were deaths. (The same procedure was used for the few persons who disappeared without explanation in recorded years.) The remaining cause-unknown exits, between ages JA 7 and JA 50, were then treated on three different assumptions: (1) that all were emigrations; (2) that all were deaths; (3) that half were migrations and half deaths in each age group. This gave low, high, and medium estimates of mortality.

As to entries, a person who came into the village during a gap and remained after the gap presents no problem. The fact of entry is evident from the first *SAC* after the gap, and the reason for the entry can usually be inferred from the person's registration as a bride, infant, servant, returned family member, or other. And the date of the entry can then be established by the same method we used to date exits in gap years.[c] But persons who both enter and exit during a gap will invariably be missed. Migrants are not likely to do this: most in-migrants were in fact brides who entered at ages when the risk of death was slight and typically remained in the village many years longer than any gap in our record. But some children registered during a gap would inevitably have died in the same period. Approximately how many births and deaths have we missed in this way?

Fortunately, in only 13 years during 1716–1830 were both the *SAC* and the *ZGC* missing; and there were only two gaps of more than a single year (1736–38 and 1782–84). Moreover, these gaps were scattered over the whole period rather than bunched (see Table 2.1). We have estimated the number of omitted births/deaths in these years on the assumption that the number for each sex in a given year was the annual average of births of that sex minus the recovered births of that sex for the year (that is, children who outlived the gap).[d] The estimated total of omitted births/deaths for all gap years is nine males and four females.

Since the unrecorded cases were so few and were scattered at considerable intervals, we ignored them. The alternative would have been to drop the gap years from the study entirely. For many purposes this would not have affected our results appreciably; but it would have complicated procedure greatly, and could possibly have distorted the estimates of completed family size, birth intervals, and mother's age at last birth. These measures all require that individual fertility histories be followed over several decades, and eliminating gap years would have entailed dropping from the population all persons whose fertile years overlapped a gap. This would have dras-

[c] Or, in the case of a birth, by counting back to the year of birth from the child's registered age.

[d] We figured the annual average of births by averaging the five nearest years of record before and after the year in question (ten years in all).

Rock Valley College - ERC

tically reduced the size of the population, especially of persons with long marriages, and it would have significantly weighted the sample toward marriages in periods without gaps.

By using all gap years, we could study fertility for all women appearing in the register, and could include all births, deaths, and migrations recovered for the gap years. However, we did have to omit the estimated 13 births/deaths occurring in gap years, as well as the 12 births mentioned earlier that *may* have been lost through "cause unknown" entries. Table 2.2 attempts to estimate the effect of both kinds of omission, singly and in combination, on the three fertility measures that are most likely to be seriously affected: mean completed family size, mean interval between births, and mother's mean age at last birth.[e] It will be seen that the combined effect of omissions on all three measures is negligible.

Recording Errors

Registration errors were frequent in Nakahara; but most of them, such as wrong characters in a name or the same age repeated for a person in two consecutive years, were trivial and easily corrected. Sudden jumps in age were especially common and, once occurring, were often perpetuated for years. We were nearly always able to correct such mistakes with considerable confidence.[f] But in twelve cases in which jumps were large (averaging 16 years), we could not decide which of the alternative ages was likely to be correct. However, these cases made only a slight difference in our life tables, as we discovered by constructing alternative tables using minimum and maximum ages at death. For simplicity, and in order not to underestimate mortality, we therefore adopted minimum

[e] The effect on crude and age-specific rates would be no greater and probably much less.

[f] By reconstructing the person's age from birth date or, in the case of immigrants or persons already present in 1717, from the first year of registration. In some cases, we simply used the age sequence that gave the most reasonable age for a person at such events as marriage, birth of first and last child, and so on. We never used age of death in making a judgment of reasonableness, however, and it is obvious from the examples above that the rule of reason worked better for women than for men.

TABLE 2.2
Effects of Interpolated Births on Fertility Measures
(Complete first marriages only)

Fertility measure	Uncorrected	Corrected for gaps	Corrected for gaps and cause-unknown entries
Mean completed family size	5.1	5.2	5.3
Mean birth interval* (years)	3.5	3.5	3.4
Mother's mean age at last birth			
Assumption 1†	37.5	37.6	37.7
Assumption 2‡	37.5	37.9	38.3

NOTE: Omitted births are assigned to complete first marriages using the proportion of all registered births that occurred in complete first marriages (328/658): 6 of 13 births lost in gap years; 6 of 12 births possibly lost by misclassification; 12 of 25 births omitted in these two ways combined.

   * Assumes that none of the recovered births were last births; thus we are overestimating the effect of recovered births on birth intervals.

   † Assumes the same proportion of last births among recovered births as that among all registered births in complete first marriages (64/328). Also assumes that the mean interval between a recovered last birth and the penultimate birth (registered last birth) was 4.2 years (the mean last registered birth interval).

   ‡ Assumes all recovered births were last births.

ages in all twelve cases. Fortunately, all these were males, so this decision did not affect the measurement of fertility.

Hidden Bias

So far we have been dealing with features of the registers that soon become evident to anyone who uses them. Some of these features, such as gap years and cause-unknown entries, are possible sources of distortion, and it is important to be aware of the nature and probable extent of the bias they introduce. But the registers may also contain hidden biases that can be detected, if at all, only by tests specifically designed to reveal them. Three biases of this kind occurred to us as possible and were tested for.

Underregistration. It is conceivable that some persons were never registered despite long residence in Nakahara. We know of no particular reason this would happen; and if it did happen, it would not necessarily bias estimates of mortality and fertility unless the underregistration was sizable and affected a particular social stratum. One way nonregistrants in Nakahara might be discovered is to consult the special lists of absentees that were made up in 1764, 1780, and 1792. These lists supposedly included all people who had left Nakahara and were known or thought to be still alive. It is clear that the lists were compiled from memory rather than from past registers, since the remembered ages and dates of departure, in a high proportion of cases, do not correspond precisely with those recorded at the time of the event; and the further back in time the departure, the more the remembered age tends to be off. If a considerable number of nonregistrants had been present in the village at any time prior to the compilation of the lists, we might hope to find them on this list of absentees made up from memory.

There are 95 persons on the absentee lists, not counting repeats, and their departures go back as far as 1740. But each of them can be unmistakably identified in earlier *SAC*'s and can be observed living for a more or less extended period in the village and then departing normally, usually for marriage. The 95 absentees include 69 women, a predominance explained by the tendency of women to marry outside the village. This is especially interesting in view of the widespread belief among researchers that females were underregistered in eighteenth-century Japan. Whatever the general case, in Nakahara few if any persons other than children (and not many of them) appear to have escaped registration for more than a year or so.

Inertia in registration. By law, as noted earlier, the annual register was supposed to be compiled by house-to-house visits, or at least by consulting househeads one by one. However, at times mistakes in ages were perpetuated from year to year in a way suggesting that some entries were simply copied from the previous year's register, with suitable changes. In this way some persons might possibly have been carried in the register for years after death or migration; and when the mistake was finally discovered, the departure may have been noted as if it had occurred in the current year. If this happened frequently, it would of course inflate the population at risk and exaggerate ages at death, leading to a possibly serious underestimate of mortality. But in that case we should find an ab-

normally large number of deaths occurring at very high ages, and
we do not: of the 450 deaths that took place in Nakahara, there
were 16 at 85 or over, which is not a suspiciously high percentage.[g]

Purposeful distortion of ages. We can think of no reason that
ages would have been intentionally exaggerated or understated, but
if either event occurred it would distort all age-specific measures. If
age were exaggerated, for example, we would underestimate
mortality in each age group by having included persons with lower
mortality risks than their normal ages would indicate. The only exception would be at the beginning of life, where the inclusion of
children under five in the over-five category would increase mortality in the latter.

We would not expect the ages of persons actually born in the
village to be intentionally distorted; such persons were registered at
JA 2 and their ages recorded consistently thereafter (except for
cases of obvious error). Immigrants are the most likely source of
misstated ages. We can check the probability of a systematic distortion of immigrants' ages by matching the age distribution of
immigrants at entry and of Nakahara emigrants at exit, on the
assumption that the ages of emigrants, who were mainly native-
born villagers, were accurate. We would expect the two distributions to be closely similar if immigrants' ages were correctly
reported. Figure 2.2 shows that the age distribution of the two
groups is nearly identical. The only notable difference is that somewhat more emigrants left at ages over 35 than immigrants who
entered over that age, but the difference is not great and is probably
largely a by-product of our accounting system for persons who left
the village to work.[h]

---

[g]The oldest inhabitant of the village, who was 67 in the first surviving *SAC* in
1717, died in 1753 at 103, according to his *SAC* age notation. However, the *ZGC*
for that year recorded his age at death as 93. We used the lower age, in accordance
with our rule of prudence when there were alternative ages and no reasonable
grounds for choosing between them.

[h]Persons who left the village to work and who either returned later or died outside the village were treated as if they had never left the village, and deaths were
treated as if they had occurred in the village. This procedure was used in order to

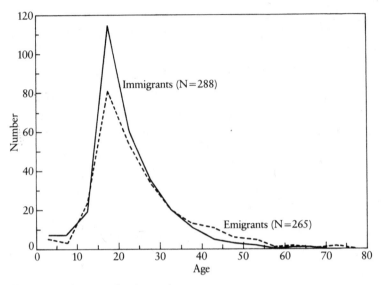

Fig. 2.2. Immigrants and emigrants by age

Tax Registers

Aside from the various population registers, the main type of document we have used from Nakahara is a tax register called *Gonengu narabi sho osameage mono menwari chō* (or MC). This listed the
landholders of the village and the value of the fields held by each,
household by household, as assessed for purposes of taxation. The
assessment, or *kokudaka*, was expressed in measures (*koku*) of rice,
or in rice equivalents where other crops were grown. Each field was
measured for size, and was graded for quality by inspections at harvest over a number of years, often including the test-harvesting of
representative squares in a field. Once the grade of land was established, the output in rice per unit of land (*tan*) could be calculated
from a table giving the productivity equivalent of each grade. Thus

obtain the maximum number of person-years and deaths for the construction of life
tables. It had the result, however, of substantially reducing both emigrations and
immigrations; and it also tended to minimize emigration in the earlier age groups
and immigration in the later ones.

from grade and size the *kokudaka* of a given field could be calculated.[3]

We have Nakahara tax registers for ten dates: 1716, 1727, 1738, 1746, 1764, 1780, 1792, 1802, 1812, and 1823. Hence we know, at intervals of approximately ten to fifteen years, the *kokudaka* of each household in Nakahara, with the exception of households occasionally omitted through oversight. This permits us to classify households by size of holding—for example, above and below median *kokudaka*—and to compare the demographic behavior of the different economic groups. Certain methodological difficulties occur when households move from one holding class to another (an event that occurs surprisingly often), but these problems can best be discussed as they arise. Here, it will be enough to say that nearly every demographic measure shows either suggestive or statistically significant differences between various groups of holders.

Nevertheless, *kokudaka* is an extremely crude index of economic and social status. For one thing, land surveys in which each field was measured and graded were expensive and technically complicated; for this reason, as well as fear of peasant resistance, they were rarely made at regular intervals. Many villages and feudal domains were not surveyed between the late seventeenth and the early nineteenth century, and to the best of our knowledge there was no land survey in Nakahara during the period 1716–1830. Over several decades, as contemporary writers repeatedly pointed out, the quality and even the size of individual fields could change radically. Consequently, the tax registers in Nakahara (and most other places) cannot be regarded as an entirely accurate reflection of landholding.[4]

Moreover, the registers tell us nothing about land that may have been held outside the village. We would expect some landholding of this kind, since we find some outsiders holding land in Nakahara.[1] Landholding across village boundaries was easy enough in the flat polder country around Nakahara, since the fields of adjoining

[1]At four dates for which we have data on outsiders—1716, 1727, 1738, and 1746—their holdings accounted, respectively, for 20, 13, 7, and 18 percent of all registered arable land in Nakahara.

villages abutted one another with no barrier of waste, forest, or mountain. So, although there may have been legal and political difficulties in transferring land ownership across boundaries, there was no physical obstacle. At the same time, only parts of a family's holdings were likely to be located outside the village. Hence there is some probability that the relative size of holdings within Nakahara may be a reasonably good guide to the relative total size of holdings, though we have no way of confirming this; and of course this general rule would not necessarily hold for particular cases.

It must be remembered, too, that the tax registers record only who owned the land, not how it was distributed for farming. Unquestionably there was considerable tenancy in Nakahara, especially after 1780, with large holders letting excess land to small holders and landless families. This is a subject we will discuss at length later. Here, we merely wish to note that as a result of tenancy some families farmed more land than the registers reflect, whereas others received income from land that they did not themselves farm.

Finally, the tax registers give no information on income from by-employment, which was substantial in many villages. We know little about the subject in Nakahara, and for this reason our impression is that the income from this source was not significant. But there was clearly some income of this kind, since young people often worked outside the village for several years before marriage. The income from this, and possibly from other nonagricultural sources, though perhaps unimportant to the village economy as a whole, may have been highly significant for the poorest families.

To summarize: the *kokudaka* data seem to point to real economic and social differences between households, since rather clear and consistent differentials in demographic behavior appear between holders of different size. This is somewhat surprising in view of the deficiencies of the tax registers; and we are inclined to think that the behavior differentials between classes may have been even sharper and more varied than our data show.

Chapter Three   The Village

At the broadest part of Honshu, the mountain systems of that long island meet in a vast, confused mass whose tallest peaks form the Japan Alps. From this snowy fastness, numerous rivers carry water down to the Pacific at Ise Bay, which at one time reached inland almost to the foothills. Over millennia the inner bay filled with sand, gravel, and clay to create the Nobi plain, which today forms an alluvial fan stretching 30 to 50 miles from the head of the bay to the mountains.

The Nobi plain in the twentieth century is one of the most densely populated parts of the country. At the beginning of the Tokugawa period, however, it was sparsely inhabited, a province of marshy grasses and water birds. Early in the seventeenth century, as a result of ditching, diking, and the skillful diversion of floodwaters to deposit silt in selected spots, islands of arable land began to form west of the Kiso River. This work was encouraged by the feudal lords of the region in order to increase the population and tax revenues of their domains. One of the most energetic rulers was Toda, *daimyō* of Ōgaki, whose fief included the fen country between the Ibi and Makita rivers; and about this time he gave local notables from the villages bordering the fens the right to bring parts of them under cultivation. These men, for the most part descended from *samurai*, had great influence with the local people, and by promising shares in land they raised the labor to create *wajū*, or polder, investing immense effort over a long period. For some years the owners typically farmed these new fields while remaining in their home villages; but gradually sheds and more substantial buildings were constructed on the reclaimed land, younger sons and brothers were settled there, and in time villages took shape.

Such a village was the settlement for which we have adopted the pseudonym "Nakahara." It lay in the middle of a polder occupied by some half-dozen new settlements at the juncture of the Ibi and the Makita and about five miles south of the castle town of Ōgaki. Ōgaki in the mid-eighteenth century was a place of perhaps ten thousand population, with a nucleus of government offices ringed by the quarters of *samurai* and townsmen, and beyond this a ragged periphery of markets, shrines, temples, and squatters' shacks. To this day the town has a countrified air. Shops are small, buildings over two stories rare, and streets potholed and dusty. Living in the shadow of Gifu, the prefectural capital to the east, and of metropolitan Nagoya somewhat farther away to the southeast, the town seems content with its role as a local commercial and administrative center.

Driving south from Ōgaki today, one turns off the concrete road after a few minutes and is suddenly away from the clutter of wayside businesses and into the country. Nakahara is a mile or so farther on by gravel road. Rice fields stretch out from its knot of houses to the bluish haze of mountains in the distance. Scattered on the immense carpet of green are the dark forms of other villages; and here and there in open spaces are schools, factories, warehouses, and transformer stations.

Houses line the gravel road of the village for several hundred yards, one house deep on one side and three or four on the other. Beside the road are other, miscellaneous structures: an antique community hall still used for grain storage; a Buddhist temple with someone asleep on the shaded porch; a village store with a bright red tobacconist's sign, set back behind a plot of cultivated land; a tiny wooden shrine containing a human figure in stone decked out in a neckerchief; an old-fashioned shallow-bottomed boat half submerged in the roadside ditch. Farther down the road, at the end of the village, is the graveyard, a rectangle of land the size of a schoolroom and crowded with upright shafts of stone.

The present number of households in the village is around 50, approximately the same as at the end of the Tokugawa period. In the past century many individuals have left the village; but few families have, and only two or three families have moved in. This number does not include the half-dozen or so families who live in recently built stucco houses with shiny blue tile roofs, which stand starkly white and new amid the rice fields a short distance from the village, each on a square of filled-in paddy. These are neither spatially nor socially a part of the village proper, whose predominantly dark color proclaims its separateness from the newcomers. The village houses are of unpainted, weathered wood, and each is surrounded by a high wooden fence or a dark-green hedge. The roofs are of black-grey tile, the interiors are dark and creaking, and the yards are simply packed earth except for occasional flowers and shrubs. Despite the presence of television aerials, automobiles, plastic carports, hand tractors, motorcycles, small trucks, washing machines, and refrigerators, the overall impression on a visitor is one of great age.

When Nakahara was founded is uncertain. It is known that in 1645 one Maki Kizaemon (a pseudonym), who would seem to have been of recent *samurai* stock, was given authority to bring a piece of land under cultivation on the present site. How the work was organized and how it went we do not know; but by 1664 a substantial amount of arable land was registered at Nakahara, though whether a settlement also existed then is doubtful. In 1717, the date of the first surviving population register, the village had a population of only 120. The families listed then give a distinct impression of recent establishment, containing relatively few married couples and few children. Many families registered were composed exclusively of brothers, or of a single parent and an adult son. These appear to have been recent branches (*bunke*) established by the nearby main families (*honke*) who had opened the land to cultivation. At any rate, we see some branching of just this kind inside Nakahara after 1717: a family head setting up a son or brother in a new house, giving him a piece of land, and sending off with him a single surviving parent, usually a mother.

During the twenty years immediately after 1717, the village grew steadily and took on a more normal appearance. Many brides came in, and nearly all the surviving single househeads of 1717 married and had children. By 1740 the total population had grown to 184, and the average household size had increased from 3 to 4. The sex ratio became less skewed in favor of males, and children made up approximately the same proportion of the population as they were to do for the rest of the century.

In the century or so after 1717, the population of Nakahara grew remarkably, especially considering that the national population was stagnant, and that arable land in the village did not expand in this period. From 120 in 1717 population grew to 284 in 1830—an annual growth rate of 0.76 percent. (The rapid increase was probably due in large part to the relatively low man/land ratio occasioned by recent settlement.) As Figure 3.1 shows, there were two great surges of growth, 1717–70 and 1795–1830, separated by a period of stagnation from 1770 to 1795.

At the same time, households increased in number and size. The average size grew from 3.0 members in 1717 to 5.4 early in the next century, and then declined to 4.9 in 1830. The number of households increased from 40 to 58. This growth was not the result of new units being added to a never-diminishing pool of old ones, as one might suppose, but was the net of appearing and disappearing households. As Figure 3.2 shows, households were almost continuously coming into and going out of existence. We do not, therefore, have in Nakahara—if anywhere in Tokugawa Japan—a village of the kind often described by historians, that is, one composed of the same group of families occupying the same land and houses for generations. There was a continuous turnover, and of the 40 families in Nakahara in 1717 only 19 were still present in 1830.

Nearly all new families came into existence by fission: an existing family would divide into a main family and a branch, partitioning property between them and presumably separating residentially. The small size of houses and the difficulty of brothers living together after the father had died were probably the major reasons for fission. In any case, 38 of 42 new families were founded in this way; the other four came into the village from outside. After division,

Population

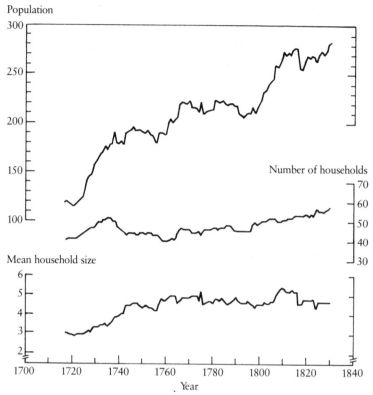

Fig. 3.1. Population, number of households, and mean household sizes in Nakahara, 1717–1830

main and branch families were distinct economic units; and branch families, who typically received much less than half the family property in a division, figured prominently among households that died out, going out of existence at about three times the rate of main families.

Families went out of existence in a variety of ways. Most often they died out biologically; occasionally they were reabsorbed into the main family; and sometimes they simply moved away from Nakahara. But never did any of these things happen so long as the family had property. It was the loss of property that made continuation as a group in the village impossible. This was the real reason

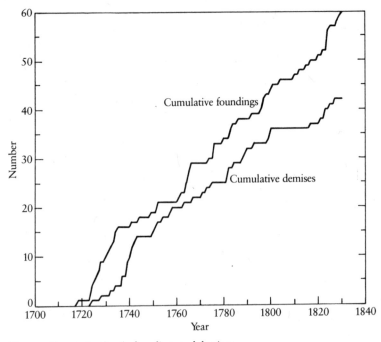

Fig. 3.2. Cumulative family foundings and demises

for a demise, even when a family died out biologically; for heirs could always be adopted or appointed posthumously by relatives when there was property to inherit.

The population of Nakahara grew exclusively or mainly from natural increase. Migration contributed little to growth and may even have taken more people from the village (mostly brides) than it brought in. We cannot be more precise owing to the 12 "cause unknown" entries for children who may either have been born in the village or have been adopted into it from outside, and to the 72 exits of persons between ages 6 and 49 who may either have died or migrated. But maximum, medium, and minimum estimates of natural increase are possible, using various assumptions concerning these problematic entries and exits (see Table 3.1). The medium estimate of natural increase, it should be noted, is probably too low: it assumes that half the 72 exits were deaths and half migrations, though all occurred at ages when migration was considerably more likely than death.

Since for the whole period births greatly exceeded deaths, and since the death rate in Nakahara was presumably high, as in other preindustrial communities, we would expect the birth rate to be very high. But in fact it is moderate to low by preindustrial standards, even after we include estimated deaths for children who were born and died without registration (see Chapter 4). Later, we will calculate age-specific fertility; but for the moment it will be enough to consider the crude birth rate, which is shown by decade in Table 3.2. Compared to rates in underdeveloped countries today, which run consistently in the 40's and 50's, the Nakahara average is distinctly low—about the same as that in eighteenth-century Sweden, where fertility was limited by restrictions on marriage, and also similar to rates for villages elsewhere in Tokugawa Japan.

The crude death rate was obviously still lower, since population was growing by natural increase (see Table 3.3). The decadal crude rate fluctuated between 18 and 32 deaths per 1,000, with a mean of 26.5 (unweighted). Moreover, these estimates of mortality are based on the probably too-pessimistic assumption that half the 72 unexplained exits were deaths.

What we know of the marshy environment of Nakahara does not

TABLE 3.1

Estimates of Natural Increase and Net Migration in Nakahara, by Period

Population change	1717–70	1771–95	1796–1830	1717–1830
Net change	+103	−12	+73	+164
Natural increase				
Minimum	+70	0	+65	+135
Medium	+85.5	+14.5	+77	+177
Maximum	+101	+29	+89	+219
Net migration				
Minimum	+2	−41	−16	−55
Medium	+17.5	−26.5	−4	−13
Maximum	+33	−12	+8	+29

NOTE: Maximum assumptions are that all 12 "cause unknown" entries were births and that none of the 72 unidentified exits were deaths. Minimum assumptions are that all 12 entries were in-migration and all 72 exits deaths. Medium assumptions are midway between these extremes.

TABLE 3.2
Adjusted Crude Birth Rate by Decade

Decade	Births per 1,000	Decade	Births per 1,000
1721–30	25	1781–90	34
1731–40	48	1791–1800	43
1741–50	40	1801–10	32
1751–60	28	1811–20	30
1761–70	43	1821–30	47
1771–80	29		

TABLE 3.3
Adjusted Crude Death Rate by Decade

Decade	Deaths per 1,000	Decade	Deaths per 1,000
1721–30	31	1781–90	32
1731–40	29	1791–1800	26
1741–50	18	1801–10	19
1751–60	31	1811–20	29
1761–70	22	1821–30	29
1771–80	26		

particularly help to explain the low mortality in the village. There were frequent complaints of stagnant water (*akusui*) in the region, a condition that must have posed a health problem, besides interfering with farming. Standing water would have bred mosquitoes, driven mice and rats to the high ground where people lived, and generally facilitated the spread of bacteria and parasites. One would expect in these conditions a high incidence of plague, cholera, typhus, typhoid, malaria, and similar ills; and, as we shall see, the age pattern of deaths in fact hints at the prevalence of such diseases.

Drainage was part of the larger problem of flood. Immense quantities of water came down from the mountains and flowed over the Nobi plain in meandering rivers, which were often diked to maintain a level above the surrounding fields. Flood was a constant threat in the polder country, where periodically one of the encircling rivers broke through or overflowed its dikes, inundating the flat, featureless country for miles around. One can still see in the vicinity today so-called water houses (*mizuya*), which were built on high platforms of stone or packed earth for storage and refuge in time of flood. But these were useful only as a last resort; they did nothing to limit the damage to houses and fields.

Beginning about 1770, a series of great drainage ditches was built along the entire length of the Nakahara polder. These collected water and carried it to the extremity of the polder downstream, where it was dumped into the encircling river. In time of flood, however, the water backed up and increased flooding upstream. Finally, after a decade of planning, a tunnel was dug to carry water under the river and thence by ditches a considerable distance downstream, to a place where the river flowed swiftly enough that the water could be discharged into it without backflow. This immense project was completed in 1785 after years of work, great expense, and public controversy, as well as the suicide of the *samurai* engineer in charge.

It hardly seems an accident that the construction of this project, during which taxes and labor contributions must have been extremely heavy, approximately coincides with the period when the population of Nakahara failed to grow (1770–95). But equally or more important in accounting for the stagnation of population may have been a series of bad crop years in the mid-1780's. There is no question, in any case, that the generation between 1770 and 1795 was a troubled time in Nakahara. Mortality was somewhat higher than before or after, there was a substantial net loss of population by migration, and between 1780 and 1792 there was a sharp increase in the concentration of landholding. After the completion of the drainage project, Nakahara seems to have enjoyed a long period of prosperity, which lasted to the end of our record in 1830. Mortality was relatively low then, roughly as many people came into the village from the outside as left, the pattern of landholding was fairly stable, and few families went out of existence.

One of the surprising features of life in Nakahara is the frequency with which land changed hands. Few holdings were composed of precisely the same fields or were exactly the same size from one

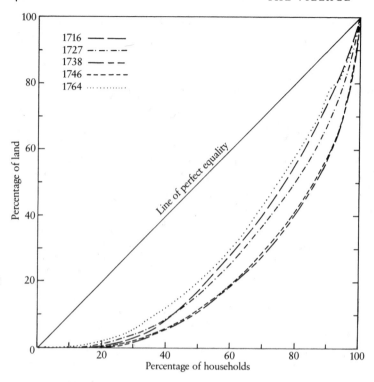

Fig. 3.3. Degree of equality of land distribution at selected dates, 1716–1823

decade to the next. Although individual holdings were thereby moving up and down the scale of size, there was an overall tendency for the ownership of land to concentrate in fewer and fewer hands.

Figure 3.3 shows the degree of equality in the distribution of land at each of ten dates for which we have tax assessments. Households are arranged by increasing size of landholding from left to right along the horizontal axis, and the vertical axis shows the percentage of total arable held. At each point on the horizontal axis we can plot the percentage of arable land held by all the holders up to that point. If land were perfectly equally distributed, the relationship would be 1 to 1: 10 percent of the holders would hold 10 percent of the land, and so on; this hypothetical situation is shown by a 45-degree straight line from the origin. The curve of actual land distri-

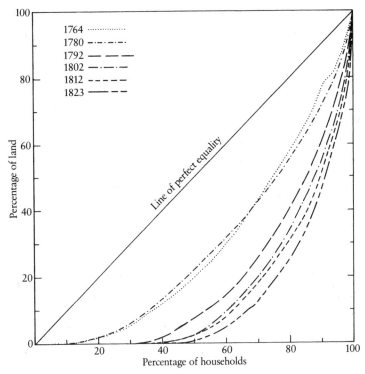

Fig. 3.3 (*continued*)

bution at a given time shows the degree of equality of distribution at that time; and the closer the curve to the diagonal line, the more nearly equal the distribution.

It will be seen that there was a severe concentration of ownership over the whole period, and that the trend intensified with every interval between tax assessments, except between 1738 and 1764. During that quarter-century, for reasons that escape us, there was a distinct lessening of inequality. The greatest intensification was in 1780–92, which overlapped work on the drainage project and contained some of the worst growing years in the century. In a decade, the proportion of entirely landless families rose from 8.5 to 28 percent.

Most of the concentration of land in these years was in the hands of the hereditary headmen, the Maki, who were descendants of the founder of Nakahara. That family's holding, already large in 1716, grew from 44 *koku* at that date to 163 *koku* in 1823, despite the foundation of three branch families with a total of 55 *koku* of land in the meantime. But we must not imagine from this one case that a few rich families became steadily richer and the rest poorer. The Maki were exceptions; more usual were families who moved up the holding scale at some times and down at others. Just as the population of the village was continuously turning over, so was the membership of various classes of holders.

One question raised by the overall concentration of landholding is whether living standards for the bulk of the population worsened as a result. Our guess is that they probably did not. For one thing, owing to the steady improvement of drainage and to general technical improvements in agriculture during the eighteenth century, in which Nakahara must have participated, the productivity of land probably rose significantly. This is suggested by the steady fall in the amount of arable land available per person, which declined from 5.4 *koku* in 1717 to 2.5 *koku* in 1823 (Table 3.4). If this fall of more than 50 percent had not been accompanied by an equal or greater rise in productivity, one would expect a substantial rise in mortality to result, but clearly this did not happen. And if productivity was in fact rising, the reduction in the amount of land held by families who were losing land would not necessarily mean a decline in their income.

Another factor is that concentration of ownership increased tenancy, and tenancy may have tended to equalize access to land. Large holders such as the Maki worked a home farm and let out additional land to tenants. Most of the additional land that came into their hands toward the end of the eighteenth century came from other large or medium holders; it could not have come in large amounts from the smaller holders. But part of the additional land, and perhaps most of it, was let in tenancy to very small holders and landless families, of whom there were always a fair number in the village. The effect of concentrated ownership and increased tenancy, therefore, may actually have been to improve the lot of the

TABLE 3.4
Arable Land per Capita Held by Nakahara Households

Date	Arable land per capita (*koku*)	Date	Arable land per capita (*koku*)
1716	5.4	1780	3.8
1727	5.2	1792	3.8
1738	4.1	1802	3.2
1746	4.0	1812	2.7
1764	3.8	1823	2.5

poorest families in the village through the loss of land by the upper and middle strata families.

One piece of evidence tending indirectly to confirm this effect is that differences in family size between small, medium, and large holders, which were very marked in the mid-eighteenth century, for all practical purposes disappeared after about 1800 (see pp. 122–24). The only explanation we can find for this remarkable change is the equalization of access to land through tenancy, together with a tendency on the part of families to adjust their size—through deliberate branching or incorporation of new members—to the labor requirements of farming.

This brings us back to a surprising feature of village life that we noted in passing a moment ago: the intense competitiveness of farming, as evidenced by the mobility of land. This quality seems to have flowed from the overwhelming importance of the family to farming, since capital in farming was relatively unimportant and little use was made of nonfamily labor. But the family unit was unstable and constantly changing. Because the process of change was universal but reacted on farming variably, with one family benefiting at the same time another suffered and with the positions of comparative advantage often being reversed later on, arable land changed hands very frequently.

From the viewpoint of the village these changes transferred land from less to more efficient farming units. But from the viewpoint of the individual family the loss of land was a matter of life and death, since families with less land were more likely to disappear as corporate residential units. Sometimes they remained in the village and died out biologically, through lower fertility and higher mortality; sometimes they emigrated. Family survival in Nakahara meant continuity with the past through occupation of the same house and the enjoyment of an acknowledged social position; and since departure from the village would interrupt this continuity, the struggle for land was a struggle for more than property. To achieve a sense of continuity with ancestors and the hope of continuity with descendants, a family would go to great lengths. This seems to us one of the dominant features of Tokugawa village life, and it is one to which we must return.

Chapter Four Mortality

WITH ROBERT T. LUNDY

T HIS CHAPTER summarizes our findings on age-specific mortality in Nakahara and compares them with data on other approximately contemporaneous rural communities, insofar as this is
possible and fruitful. The comparisons lead to no firm conclusions;
but they do suggest that mortality in Nakahara was not radically
different from that in other Tokugawa villages for which there are
estimates, though there are good reasons to believe that it may have
been rather low in comparison to mortality in preindustrial French
parishes.

High, Low, and Medium Estimates

A life table is a convenient way to present estimates of age-
specific mortality.[1] We constructed three versions of all life tables
presented here, using different assumptions about the 72 cause-
unknown disappearances that are the major source of uncertainty
in our mortality data: the *low* assumption, that all were cases of
migration; the *medium*, that half were deaths and half migrations;
and the *high*, that all were deaths. Table 4.1 shows these estimates
for Nakahara in 1717–1830, with both sexes combined and using
five-year age groups.

There are two reasons for believing that our lowest estimate of
mortality (i.e. highest life expectancy) is nearest the truth. First, in
preparing our data we assumed that all unidentified disappearances
under JA 7 or over JA 50 were deaths; thus we are concerned here
only with the ages in between, for which, judging from exits for

TABLE 4.1
Nakahara Life Tables, Both Sexes Combined, 1717–1830

	Low		Medium		High	
Standard Age	Survivors per 1,000 (1x)	Life expectancy (years)	Survivors per 1,000 (1x)	Life expectancy (years)	Survivors per 1,000 (1x)	Life expectancy (years)
1	1,000	48.2	1,000	45.7	1,000	43.4
5	874	51.0	872	48.1	871	45.6
10	836	48.2	830	45.5	825	42.9
15	805	44.9	791	42.6	778	40.4
20	776	41.5	755	39.5	735	37.6
25	740	38.4	710	36.9	681	35.4
30	713	34.8	670	33.9	630	33.0
35	682	31.2	631	30.8	585	30.4
40	651	27.6	600	27.3	554	27.0
45	613	24.1	562	24.0	515	23.8
50	564	21.0	514	21.0	469	20.9
55	506	18.2	460	18.2	419	18.2
60	453	15.0	412	15.0	375	15.0
65	408	11.4	371	11.4	337	11.4
70	321	8.8	292	8.8	265	8.8
75	201	7.5	183	7.5	167	7.5
80	124	5.7	113	5.7	103	5.7
85	50	5.6	45	5.6	41	5.6

known causes, emigration was far more likely than death.[a] Second, in comparing our life tables with the Coale-Demeny model life tables, the worst fit using the low estimate of mortality was far better than the best fit using the medium or high estimates (see Appendix A). With the exception of Table 4.1 (and elsewhere as specified), we have therefore presented only the low estimate of mortality.

The outstanding feature of this life table is the generally moderate level of mortality (more on this later). Another peculiarity is the relatively high mortality during the middle years of life as compared to what one would expect on the basis of mortality at the older ages. This is apparent in Figure 4.1, which graphs the number

[a]For the entire period 1717–1830, this intermediate group had 248 emigrations, 159 deaths, and 66 unidentified departures. The population used in subsequent life tables treats persons working outside the village as though they were in the village, provided they remain registered in the village and hence under observation. We call this the *de jure* population. See Appendix A for data.

of Nakahara male deaths per 1,000 by five-year age groups in comparison with the same measure for two Coale-Demeny model populations in which mortality is at the same general level as in Nakahara. Quite aside from a few jagged irregularities (the result of random variation with small numbers), it will be seen that the Nakahara curve is notably flatter than those of the two model populations. After reaching nadir the models move up steeply, whereas the Nakahara curve moves laterally for a time and turns up definitely only at age 35. The mortality curve for females in Nakahara shows this same flatness.

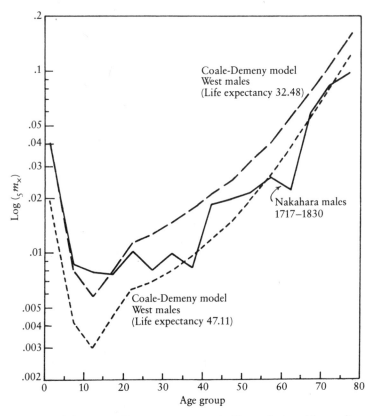

Fig. 4.1. Nakahara mortality patterns compared with standard model mortality patterns

Causes of death have characteristic age patterns, and from the mortality curve of a sufficiently large population it is theoretically possible to estimate the relative importance of different causes. The Nakahara population is too small for this, but the pronounced flatness of the curve may indicate that infectious and parasitic diseases (S. H. Preston's group 2)[2] were a more frequent cause of death in Nakahara than they would be in a modern population at the same level of mortality. Neither the "modern" degenerative diseases nor the diarrheal disorders so commonly found in Latin America and Asia today appear important in Nakahara. Both of these produce a strongly rising rate of death with age and, if widespread, would have given a curve more like those of the model populations. Tuberculosis (Preston's group 1) might be thought important on the basis of the curve alone, but it is unlikely to appear on a significant scale in a rural Japanese environment in the eighteenth and early nineteenth centuries.

Sex

In modern societies females usually have a distinct advantage over males in life expectancy, though in less economically developed societies and in populations with high mortality generally the advantage is far less pronounced. Indeed, some early life tables for India and Ceylon (and, interestingly, one for Ireland) show a reversal of the differential; and it has been suggested that historical populations might be found that show a consistent male advantage. However, this is clearly not the case in Nakahara. Females had an advantage over males in life expectancy at any given age (see Table 4.2). Over the whole period 1717–1830 female deaths per 1,000 averaged about 84 percent of the male rate (and only 70.5 percent in 1717–49)—a greater advantage than one would expect on the basis of the most closely comparable Coale-Demeny model life tables.[b]

[b] The ratio of female to male deaths also favored females over shorter periods: 0.705 in 1717–49; 0.932 in 1750–74; 0.886 in 1775–99; and 0.828 in 1800–1830.

TABLE 4.2
Life Expectancy by Sex, 1717–1830

Age	Life expectancy	
	Male	Female
1	46.1	50.8
5	49.7	52.6
10	46.7	50.0
25	37.0	40.1
40	26.1	29.4
60	14.6	15.4

Socioeconomic Status

We can also break down mortality by size of landholding to discover whether the life expectancy of large holders was materially better than that of small holders. Unfortunately, we must be content with only a twofold division—above and below a median holding size of 12 *koku*—since a finer breakdown results in groups too small to use. We classed each person in the record as a large or small holder for each year of life (see Appendix B). The two groups tended to merge at the 12-*koku* boundary; however, the average size of holdings in the large-holding group was nearly four times that in the small-holding group. Where a person fell into both groups during the course of his life, we attributed to each group the person-years lived in it.[3]

For the entire period, life expectancy at age 1 for each sex and landholding class in Nakahara was as follows:

	Female	Male
Large holdings	52.5 yrs.	49.2 yrs.
Small holdings	48.2	42.8
All holdings	50.8	46.1

It is not surprising that large holders of both sexes enjoyed a pronounced advantage in longevity. The advantage was especially large for males, possibly because men's workloads in the two classes were sharply different and women's were not; but this is sheer speculation.

When we compare males and females in the same holding class, we find a large female advantage for the whole period in the small-holding class only. This advantage was due in large part to the period before 1764; after that date females still enjoyed an advantage in both classes, but the extreme advantage among small holders disappeared (see Table 4.3). This was not because female mortality rose in the later period, but because male mortality declined. The implied improvement of conditions among small holders strengthens our belief, already mentioned, that the increase in tenancy in the late eighteenth century may have improved the economic status of small holders and landless families (see pp. 43–44).

We noted earlier that our data on landholding are a very imperfect guide to family income: they probably reflect out-of-date rather than current assessments of fields; they take no account of land that may have been held outside the village; and they tell us nothing about land held in tenancy or about nonfarm income. Given these shortcomings, we would not necessarily expect to find any significant differences in mortality between the two classes of holders. That we do find them, for both sexes, is gratifying. It suggests that the tax registers actually do reflect to some extent real economic differences between families—though probably to a lesser extent after the late eighteenth century than before. This prompted us to divide the population by holding size for other demographic measures in addition to mortality.

Mortality over Time

We would expect mortality to fluctuate over time; and as we found earlier, the crude death rate did move up and down by decade. To discover whether there was any long-term trend in mortality, we compiled age-specific death rates for periods of approximately 25 years and calculated life tables and standardized death rates from them. Although the results show a very slight tendency toward lower mortality over time, it does not seem significant; and in any case the overall trend is less marked than the variations from one period to another. Standardized deaths per 1,000 were 20.1 in 1717–49; 17.6 in 1750–74; 20.3 in 1775–99;

TABLE 4.3
Mortality Ratios in Nakahara by Economic
Status and Sex

Ratio	1717–1830	1764–1830
Large holding/ small holding		
Female	0.839	0.839
Male	0.509	0.965
Female/male		
Large holding	1.06	0.827
Small holding	0.644	0.853

NOTE: Ratios were standardized on the age distribution of total person-years for both sexes combined.

and 16.0 in 1800–1830. Taking the rate of 18.2 for the whole period 1717–1830 as 1.000, the corresponding ratios for the four subperiods were 1.104, 0.967, 1.115, and 0.879, presenting a rather clear sequence of high, low, high, and low mortality.[c]

To some extent, this sequence can probably be explained by the tendency in preindustrial populations—or indeed, in any population exposed to communicable diseases—for mortality to vary in a cyclical manner. Periods of high mortality come about when a relatively large proportion of the population has never been exposed to a particular disease. The survivors are left with immunity to the disease, and until a relatively large pool of new, unexposed population builds up the disease will not find a favorable environment for wide dissemination; hence mortality will be lower. When a sufficient pool has built up again, a new epidemic may strike. To the extent that conditions favoring the spread of disease may force several epidemic cycles to be more or less in phase with each other, mortality for all causes will thus tend to follow a similar cyclic path.

Beyond this, however, specific causes for the sequence seen in Nakahara suggest themselves. The high mortality of the first period

[c] Standardized on age distribution of total person-years for both sexes combined. It should be noted that these calculations do not include an adjustment for unregistered infant mortality and are therefore lower than the crude rates by decade cited in Chapter 3.

would seem to reflect the hard work of ditching and diking, as well as the primitive and unhealthy drainage conditions that marked the early years of settlement. The succeeding period of low mortality may similarly indicate the amelioration of these conditions with time. In the third period mortality rose to an all-time high, partly as a result of the heavy burden of constructing the drainage system under the Ibi River and partly as a result of a series of poor harvests that took a heavy toll of life over much of Japan in the 1780's. The last period, during which mortality was at its lowest, may have benefited from the completion of the Ibi drainage system, and perhaps also from the surprising effect of increased tenancy in putting more farmland under the direct management of the poorest families. But it must be admitted that these are very fragile inferences.

Mortality Below Age One

So far the data presented include no information on death before age 1. This omission, which results from the peculiarities of To-kugawa birth registration, is unfortunate on several counts. Never-theless, it is possible to estimate infant mortality by fitting our life table above age 1 to the Coale-Demeny model life tables and pro-jecting mortality backward from age 1 to age 0. This procedure is not without pitfalls. Identification of the appropriate model may be faulty, and a close fit above age 1 gives no absolute guarantee of a close fit between 1 and 0. It does give some probability of such a fit, however, and an estimate of infant mortality in this way is in-comparably better than one based on the general level of mortality only.

Appendix B explains how the most appropriate Coale-Demeny model was chosen. Here, it is sufficient to note that the model "North" population gave much the best fit, but that on the other hand infectious diseases such as afflicted Nakaharans are more characteristic of the "East" population than the "North." Since "East" also had the higher infant mortality, the exclusive use of "North" seemed likely to result in an underestimate. We therefore used "North" and "East" to obtain respectively low and high esti-mates, then averaged the two for a medium estimate of infant deaths per 100 births. The medium estimate came to 15.7 for females and 22.2 for males.

This enabled us to estimate life expectancy at birth for our low, medium, and high life tables. It should be recalled that these were based on different assumptions about the 72 cause-unknown departures, and that the low mortality estimate is probably nearest the truth. The estimates for both sexes combined over the entire period 1717–1830 were: low, 43.2 years; medium, 40.7 years; high, 38.2 years.

Comparisons

Assuming our estimates of life expectancy are roughly accurate, how does mortality in Nakahara compare with that in other Tokugawa villages in the eighteenth century? Table 4.4 shows the life expectancy at age 1 in Nakahara and in five other villages for which we have estimates of age-specific mortality that appear to be derived by methods comparable to our own. Our figure for Nakahara is close to that for four of the villages and rather higher than that for the fifth. From so limited a sample no far-reaching conclusions are warranted, but it seems that mortality in Nakahara was not uniquely low for Tokugawa Japan.

Tables 4.5 and 4.6 compare relevant mortality data for Nakahara with those for contemporaneous English and French parishes for which there are comparable estimates. It will be seen that mortality in Nakahara for ages 1–14 was about the same as in Colyton, England, and generally somewhat lower than in the French parishes. Also, the pattern of death in Nakahara for these ages resembled Colyton more than the French communities. The probability of death was lower than in France in the 1–4 age group but declined less sharply in the next two age groups; indeed, in Nakahara and Colyton there was little difference in probability of death between the 5–9 and 10–14 age groups. Life expectancy at birth in Nakahara was about the same as in Colyton in its best period and higher than in the French parishes. The advantage over France was largely, though not entirely, due to the lower child mortality just noted. If we compare life expectancies at age 10 rather than at

TABLE 4.4

Life Expectancy at Age 1 in Tokugawa Villages

Village	Male expectancy (years)	Female expectancy (years)
Nakahara, 1717–1830	46.1	50.8
Iinuma, 1711–81*	41.8	39.7
Fujito, 1800–1810, 1825–35	48.8	51.5
Nishijō, 1773–1800	34.6	34.4
Nishikata, 1782–96	44.0	59.2
Yokouchi, 1726–75	42.7	44.0

SOURCES: Hayami, Kinsei nōson, p. 204; "Tono ichi sanson no jinkō tōkei," p. 28; "Nōshū Nishijō mura no jinkō shiryō," p. 181. Hanley, "Fertility, Mortality, and Life Expectancy," p. 139.
* All dates except those for Nakahara refer to birth cohorts. The figures for Fujito and Nishikata are unweighted averages of estimates by Hanley for five-year periods.

TABLE 4.5

Probability of Death Among Children in Nakahara
and in Selected European Parishes

| Village | Probability of death at age | | |
	1–4 yrs.	5–9 yrs.	10–14 yrs.
Crulai, Fr.			
1688–1719	.105	.072	.027
1720–75	.138	.084	.026
Brittany and Anjou, Fr.			
1740–49	.190	.095	.050
1750–59	.177	.102	.047
1760–69	.171	.090	.063
Tourouvre-au-Perche, Fr.			
1670–1719	.220	.082	.043
1720–69	.156	.066	.031
Colyton, Eng.			
1538–99	.080	.027	.021
1600–1649	.093	.050	.044
1650–99	.113	.065	.035
1700–1746	.082	.023	.023
1750–1837	.075	.028	.020
Nakahara			
1717–1830	.127	.043	.037

SOURCES: Gautier and Henry, La Population de Crulai, pp. 162, 190–91; Charbonneau, Tourouvre-au-Perche, p. 194; Wrigley, "Mortality in Preindustrial England: The Example of Colyton, Devon, Over Three Centuries," pp. 558, 574; Blayo and Henry, "Données démographiques sur la Bretagne et l'Anjou de 1740 à 1829," p. 264.

TABLE 4.6
*Life Expectancy at Age 0 and Age 10: Nakahara and
Selected European Parishes*

Village	Life expectancy in years	
	At age 0	At age 10
Crulai, Fr.		
1675–1775	30.3	37.6
Brittany and Anjou, Fr.		
1740–49	28.2	41.5
1750–59	31.3	43.9
1760–69	30.6	42.7
Tourouvre-au-Perche, Fr.		
1670–1719	25.0	36.9
1720–69	33.1	43.0
Colyton, Eng.		
1538–1624	43.2	*
1625–99	36.9	*
1700–1774	41.8	*
Nakahara		
1717–1830	43.2†	48.2†

SOURCES: Our computations from data given by the sources cited for
Table 4.5.
* Not available.
† Low estimates of mortality. European figures are medium where high
and low estimates are also available.

birth, the difference narrows considerably, without disappearing
entirely.

All in all, Nakahara's mortality appears to have been rather low
as compared to all the European communities except Colyton, with
which it was on a par. This is rather different from our initial expectation based on Nakahara's seemingly unhealthy environment and
on the assumption that Japanese living standards in the eighteenth
century were lower and mortality therefore higher than in Western
Europe at the same time. One possible reason for Nakahara's surprisingly low mortality lies in its fertility. We shall see in Chapter 5
that registered age-specific marital fertility was well under the level
of most European parishes, and there are grounds for thinking that
this was because fertility was restrained by the widespread practice

of infanticide shortly after birth (which meant that the victims were never registered as births or deaths).

Infanticide could have contributed to low mortality in the registered population in several ways: the selective elimination of visibly weak or deformed infants; the restraint of population to numbers generally within the capacity of the village to support; some matching of family size to family resources; the particularly severe restraint of fertility in bad times; less wear and tear on mothers; and less infection because of smaller families. Although these effects are wholly speculative, the practice of infanticide is not. It can reasonably be inferred from patterns of fertility in Nakahara that are, or seem to be, otherwise inexplicable.

Chapter Five   Fertility and Infanticide

WITH ROBERT Y. ENG

WE HAVE SEEN that the crude birth rate in Nakahara, as well as in other Japanese villages for which we have figures, was on the low side for a preindustrial population. This measure may be misleading, however, since it takes no account of the age structure of the population or the proportion married of those in the reproductive ages. We turn, therefore, to age-specific marital fertility—the number of children born during a year per 1,000 married women in various five-year age groups—for a measure that will control for both age and marital status.

Table 5.1 compares age-specific marital fertility in Nakahara and in a number of contemporaneous Japanese villages and European parishes. To make the estimates as nearly comparable as possible, we have adjusted the figures in each Japanese age group for births lost through unregistered "infant mortality" at an estimated rate of 20 percent (see pp. 54–55). Two things stand out in the table. First, marital fertility in Nakahara was about median for the Japanese villages for which we have estimates. Second, it was distinctly low compared to the European parishes, with two exceptions: Colyton in 1647–1719, when there is strong evidence of the practice of some form of family limitation; and Thézels–St. Sernin, in a region of puzzlingly low fertility in southwestern France.[1]

Fertility was obviously lower in Nakahara than in any of the other European communities (including Colyton at a comparable period). This can be seen in the last column of the table, which shows the number of children a woman would have if she remained married from age 20 to age 49 and bore children in each age group

TABLE 5.1
Age-Specific Marital Fertility in Selected European and Japanese Communities

(Births per 1,000 woman-years)

Place and period	Age group							Total fertility*
	15–19	20–24	25–29	30–34	35–39	40–44	45–49	
Colyton, Eng.								
1647–1719	500	346	395	272	182	104	020	6.6
1770–1837	500	441	361	347	270	152	022	8.0
Crulai, Fr.								
1674–1742	320	419	429	355	292	142	010	8.2
Le Mesnil–Beaumont, Fr.								
1740–99	452	524	487	422	329	135	017	9.6
Thézels–St. Sernin, Fr.								
1700–1792	208	393	326	297	242	067	000	6.6
Meulan, Fr.								
1660–1739	585	519	507	503	379	157	014	10.4
1740–89	492	493	477	403	294	111	015	9.0
Anhausen, Ger.								
1692–1799	n.a.	472	496	450	355	173	037	9.9
Yokouchi, Japan								
Before 1700†	204	382	358	266	264	164	028	7.3
1701–50†	168	275	240	232	146	071	026	5.0
1751–1800†	188	205	226	161	116	078	010	4.0
After 1800†	306	264	231	202	092	042	011	4.2
Kando-shinden, Japan								
After 1800†	471	531	351	269	225	138	016	7.7
Nishijō, Japan								
1773–1835†	321	399	356	315	251	121	032	7.4
Nakahara								
1717–1830	214	326	304	300	221	122	034	6.5

SOURCES: Wrigley, "Family Limitation," p. 89; Gautier and Henry, *La Population de Crulai*, p. 105; Ganiage, *Trois villages*, p. 82; Valmary, *Familles paysannes*, p. 120; Lachiver, *La Population de Meulan*, p. 152; John Knodel, "Two-and-a-Half Centuries of Demographic History," p. 369; Hayami, *Kinsei nōson*, p. 218; Hayami, "Demographic Analysis," p. 78; Hayami, "Jinkō gakuteki," p. 182.

* Computed from ages 20 to 49.
† Birth cohorts of mothers.

at the average rate of all married women in that age group.[2] Using Nakahara's total fertility as an index of 100, the ratios were 123 for Colyton in 1770–1837, 126 for Crulai, 148 for Le Mesnil–Beaumont, 152 for Anhausen, and 160 for Meulan in 1660–1739 (138 in 1740–89). To use a graphic approach, Figure 5.1 compares age-specific marital fertility in Nakahara and in two French parishes representing cases of relatively high and low fertility for that country. The Nakahara curve, it will be seen, is at about the same level as that of Thézels–St. Sernin (low fertility) and much below that of Crulai (high fertility).

The Problem

The remainder of this chapter is addressed to the question of *why* marital fertility was relatively low in Nakahara. We argue that the primary reason was the practice of infanticide, less as a desperate act in the face of poverty than as a form of family planning. But before turning to the evidence for this contention, it will be useful to say something about two other possible causes: low female fecundity, and the practice of some form of birth control other than infanticide.

We know of no particular reason why fecundity should be low in Nakahara (or other Japanese villages), unless as a result of chronic malnutrition or disease. If either of these conditions obtained, we should expect mortality to be high; but, in fact, mortality in Nakahara was at about the same level as in Colyton in England and rather lower than in the French parishes. Nor was Nakahara's low mortality limited mainly to males; if anything, female mortality was slightly lower. So, though we cannot exclude the possibility of low female fecundity, we have reason to think it was probably not a significant factor.

Nor can we exclude the possibility that some form of birth control other than infanticide was practiced. However, the shape of Nakahara's age-specific fertility curve in Figure 5.1 is of a kind usually associated with the absence of birth control. Where birth control is not practiced, the woman's age is the preponderant factor in fertility, which is therefore independent of the length of marriage;

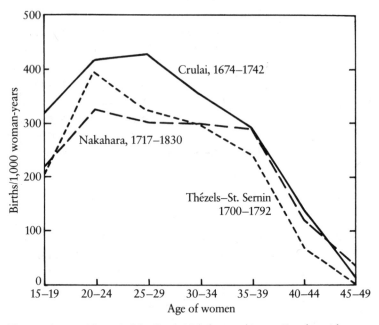

Fig. 5.1. Age-specific marital fertility in Nakahara and in two French parishes

consequently, fertility declines slowly at the early ages, then ever more rapidly as fecundity falls and the proportion of infertile couples increases. This gives a convex curve of the kind we see in Nakahara. When birth control is widespread, by contrast, couples tend to concentrate childbearing in the early years of marriage, stopping procreation when they reach the usually small number of children desired. Thus fertility declines sharply with the length of marriage and may be quite low even for young women. Age-specific fertility therefore shows a curve of the kind illustrated in Figure 5.2.[3]

Finally, it is well known that great differences in marital fertility exist between different populations in the absence of birth control. This is probably caused by different spacing between births as a result of variations in the waiting period after birth before the resumption of sexual relations, the length of suckling, and physiological differences governing the reappearance of ovulation after confinement.[4] Fertility in Nakahara may have been affected by some combination of these factors; we have no way of knowing. But it was almost certainly low in part because of infanticide.

There is an immense amount of legal and literary evidence for abortion and infanticide in Tokugawa Japan,[5] though none to our knowledge places either practice specifically in Nakahara. During the eighteenth century, *daimyō* governments repeatedly prohibited both actions, seeing them as the major inhibitors of population growth. Moralists railed against both infanticide and abortion, frequently running these distinct terms together as if they had a common moral significance. Abortion was apparently more widely practiced in the towns, where there were skilled specialists; but both practices appeared in both town and countryside, and seemingly among all classes. Contemporary writers were inclined to be lenient with the poor, whose circumstances presumably drove

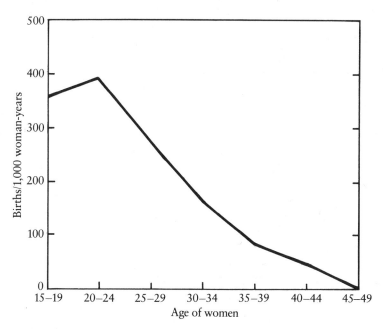

Fig. 5.2. Age-specific marital fertility in a community practicing family limitation (data from Geneva, Switzerland, for wives of husbands born 1700–1749)

them to these acts. The major accusations were directed at families in comfortable circumstances—*samurai* and merchants, as well as substantial farmers—who were said to limit children merely to increase their own ease or to improve the prospects of the children whom they chose to raise.

Infanticide is consistent, in theory at least, with the Nakahara fertility curve. If the act took place at birth, as contemporary writers say it did, the victims would never appear in the population registers; if it also occurred frequently, registered fertility would be extremely low, not only because of the eliminated births, but also because of the associated sterile periods of pregnancy. At the same time, the fertility curve would in all probability be convex. Infanticide is the only form of birth limitation (or strictly speaking, birth negation) that permits control over the sex of offspring, an advantage that no society using it would be likely to forgo entirely. And if children of the unwanted sex were sometimes eliminated, one would expect extremely long average intervals between births. As long as there were not too many very small families, childbearing would be widely spread over the fertile years of marriage; fertility would therefore tend to vary with a woman's age rather than the length of her marriage, and so would describe a convex curve.[a]

There is no way to detect abortion specifically in the Nakahara registers; but infanticide, if sex-selective, would leave many traces. What follows is an analysis of just such traces, which lead us to believe that infanticide was widely practiced in the village—and moreover, practiced less as part of a struggle for survival than as a way of planning the sex composition, sex sequence, spacing, and ultimate number of children.

Sex Bias

We initially assumed that infanticide in Nakahara would have been practiced exclusively or mainly against females, and that evi-

---

[a] The argument here is not that infanticide must always result in a convex fertility curve, only that it may sometimes do so. If infanticide were commonly resorted to only after several children had been born, being used increasingly thereafter, the practice would presumably yield a concave curve. (However, the total fertility would still be lower than that of a community with uncontrolled birth.)

dence of this would appear in the sex ratio of registered births. But this was not the case: a sex ratio of 114 males per 100 females in 652 recorded births could not be considered abnormally high. We observed, however, certain variations in sex ratio by birth order which ultimately led us to infer that infanticide was practiced against both sexes;[b] and further, that married couples had a marked tendency to have a next child of the sex underrepresented in their present family.

This tendency was evident only after the second birth; there seems to have been no general sex preference for the first two births. The subsequent preference can be seen both in complete first marriages—that is, first marriages for both partners that lasted through the wife's age 45—and in all first marriages, in the following way. Consider each married couple as a distinct case of marriage at each birth of a child when two or more previous children are registered in the household; thus a couple with six children all living and registered in Nakahara would appear as four different families in the sample, once at each birth after the second. Now divide these statistical families into three groups according to the sex of the previous children: those with predominantly male children (PM), those with predominantly females (PF), and those with an equal number of both sexes (M = F).[c] Then calculate the sex ratio of the next children born in each group. For complete first marriages only, our results were:

Existing children	Next child		
	M	F	Sex ratio
PM	30	45	67
M = F	31	21	148
PF	38	19	200

---

[b] Almost invariably, from the third birth on, odd birth orders showed a marked excess of males, and even birth orders either no bias or a slight excess of females:

Birth order	M	F	Sex ratio	Birth order	M	F	Sex ratio
3	53	43	123	7	11	10	110
4	39	40	98	8	3	6	50
5	35	18	194	9	2	1	200
6	19	19	100	10	0	1	0

[c] Includes all living siblings registered with the family at the time of birth of the next child. We excluded from the sample one birth of fraternal twins of opposite sex.

If the sex of the next child was independent of that of the previous children, the ratio of male to female births ought to have been about the same in each group of families. The ratios in the various groups, however, differ significantly from one another; and the chance of differences of this magnitude occurring independently of the sex of previous children is considerably less than 1 in 100. Also, the sex ratio in two of the groups, *PM* and *PF*, is significantly different from the "normal" human birth ratio of 102 male to 100 female.[6] We must suppose, therefore, that the sex of the next child was to some extent a matter of choice, enforced by infanticide; it would also seem that families tended to eliminate infants of the sex already predominant, and to eliminate girls somewhat more often than boys. Otherwise, it is quite inexplicable that families with predominantly male children tended to have a female as the next child by a ratio significantly different from normal; that those where females predominated tended to have males by a ratio also significantly different from normal; and that those with an equal number of both sexes, though tending to have more males than females, did not do so by a significant margin.

The results are similar when the sample is extended to include all first marriages:

Existing children	Next child		
	M	F	Sex ratio
PM	47	65	72
M = F	42	25	168
PF	55	32	172

This sample gives a less smooth rise in sex ratio from *PM* to *M = F* to *PF*. But in all groups the sex ratio of the next child was significantly different from a normal 102, and again, the differences in sex ratio between the three groups were statistically significant ($p < 0.004$).[7] It seems likely, therefore, that in both complete and incomplete marriages the parents' decision to keep or to "return" (as the euphemism had it) a newborn baby depended in part on the sex of the infant and in part on that of previous children.

We can test this inference further by dividing all first marriages into five categories rather than the three just used, thus permitting a distinction between predominant (*P*) and heavily predominant (*HP*) families for each sex.[d] If families in fact selected the sex of the next child on the basis of the sex of existing children, they should have favored the underrepresented sex by a greater margin when the imbalance was greater. The distinction between *HP* and *P* at some points in the birth order requires a degree of subjective judgment, which makes some difference in the results. But the subjective choice is a narrow one, and we have tried to minimize it by using the set of definitions that gives the fewest small cells.

Using the set so chosen, the 67 balanced families of course remain as before. But we find that *HPM* families favored females at the next birth more strongly than *PM* families; and that *HPF* families favored males more strongly than *PF* families (though in this case the difference cannot be regarded as significant, owing to the small number of *HPF* families). Nevertheless, the preferences run in the right direction:

Existing children	Next child		
	M	F	Sex ratio
HPM	13	19	68
PM	34	46	74
M = F	42	25	168
PF	48	30	160
HPF	7	2	350

The only irregularity here is that *M = F* families opted for males about as often (168) as *PF* families (160). This is probably not the result of sampling error, given the size of the numbers in the cells. One possible but wholly speculative explanation would be that the *M = F* group contained more sex-selecting families than the *PF* group; if so, since the next birth was bound to upset a sex-balanced sibling set, the *M = F* group might opt for males about as strongly as the less selective *PF* group.[e]

---

[d]Categories were defined as follows, on the basis of sibling sex division. *P* families included the ratios 2–0, 2–1, 3–1, 3–2, 4–2, 4–3, 5–2, 5–3, 5–4, 6–2, 6–3, and 7–2. *HP* families were 3–0, 4–0, 4–1, 5–0, 5–1, 6–0, 6–1, 7–0, 7–1, 8–0, 8–1, and 9–0.

[e]If we change our subjective choice slightly (and increase the very small *HPF* sample) by moving the smaller families with 2F/no M or 3F/1M from the *PF* category

Adoption

An alternative to infanticide as an explanation of the unbalanced selection of the sex of a next child is that infants were commonly adopted but registered as natural children of the adopting parents, and that such adoptions were commonly sex-selective: that is, the adopting parents often took an infant of the sex already underrepresented among their children.[f] We have tentatively rejected this possibility, for several reasons. (1) Sex-selective adoption would not explain low fertility unless considerably more children were adopted out of Nakahara than were adopted in from the outside. (2) It is difficult to understand a couple adopting when they already had two or more children living, and often had many years of fertility left as well. (3) We can find no contemporary literary or legal evidence of specifically *sex-selective* adoption, or any mention of such a practice in ethnographic literature.[g] (4) Infanticide would explain lower fertility, not only in Nakahara but potentially in other villages as well; in addition, it is known to have been widely practiced. (5) Adoptions listed as such in the Nakahara registers were almost exclusively male and nearly all of children over age 12; but if sex-selective infant adoptions were common, we should expect to find a fair number of registered adoptions of young children of both sexes.

Overall, there were 45 registered adoptions in Nakahara. All but one of the adoptees were males, and only three (at JA 2, 6, and 7) could be considered young children. The mean age of adoptees coming from inside the village was 17.4, and it was 26.4 for adoptees from outside. Of the 20 adoptions that were into Nakahara families—where we can surmise the purpose of the adoption from

---

to the *HPF*, we obtain new totals for the subsequent birth: 19 M and 16 F for the *PF* group (sex ratio 119); and 36 M to 16 F for the *HPF* (sex ratio 225). The irregularity represented by the *M* = *F* group ratio of 168 as compared to the *PF* ratio then becomes more striking.

[f]We are indebted to Sidney Crawcour and Ronald Dore for this suggestion.

[g]We know of no contemporary legal or literary evidence for sex-selective infanticide either; but this is not surprising, since infanticide was illegal and adoption was not.

the composition of the adopting family—it seems probable that all but one were intended either to provide a male heir where there was none or to provide a husband for a daughter or a female family head. The 20 break down as follows:

In nine cases: no male heir; adoptee married daughter, widowed daughter-in-law, or sister of family head.

In four cases: no male heir, no female available for marriage in adopting family. In one of these cases an adopted son already had his own wife and son.

In three cases a female family head married an adoptive husband.

In two cases a female family head with no son adopted one.

In two cases a son was adopted when an adult son was already present in the family. One of these adoptees, who already had a wife and three children of his own, eventually inherited the family headship.

Children Born After the Death of a Child

If parents in fact selected the sex of children in order to get approximately the sex mix in offspring they wished, one would suppose that when a child died they would tend to have a next child of the same sex as the deceased. To our astonishment, the opposite was the case in Nakahara: there was a significant tendency for the next child to be of the opposite sex from the deceased (see Table 5.2).[8] That is, families losing a male and left with predominantly female children nonetheless tended to have a female next, and vice versa. This tendency holds even when one controls for the sex of the surviving siblings. Perhaps replacement by a child of the same sex was thought challenging or offensive to the powers who had taken away the deceased one, though this is pure speculation.[h] What is certain is that this surprising behavior went against the

[h] The objection has been made that this assumes an absurdity, namely, that a child of the wrong sex was killed in order to preserve it from harm. But presumably infanticide was committed not primarily in the interest of its victim but of someone else— family, mother, siblings, etc. In any case, it is not necessarily absurd to think of an infant's being killed to protect it: one of the modern arguments for abortion is that the potential child is better off than if raised unwanted.

TABLE 5.2
Sex of Next Child Born After Death of a Child,
All First Marriages

Sex of deceased child	M/F distribution of next children born			
	In *PM* sets	In *M = F* sets	In *PF* sets	Total
All sibling sets*				
Male	2/3	3/9	4/10	9/22
Female	6/3	8/2	4/1	18/6
Sibling sets of two or more				
Male	2/3	2/9	1/2	5/14
Female	5/3	4/1	4/1	13/5

NOTE: We include all cases where two or more children of the same sex died before the next birth, but exclude three cases where two or more children of different sexes had died. All categories of sibling sets in the table are determined by the living children at the time of the next birth, i.e., by the sex composition of the set *after* a child has died.

  * This includes the sets with one or no child that were omitted in earlier calculations; null sets are counted in the *M = F* group. The reason for this is that we are primarily interested in the relationship between sex of deceased child and sex of next child, and introduce sibship composition only as a control variable. As can be seen, leaving out the childless or single-child families does not alter the general picture.

general tendency to balance sexes, and that otherwise this tendency would have been still stronger.[1]

Limitation of Family Size

Sex selection was probably not the only aim of infanticide in Nakahara. An equally important aim, no doubt, was family limitation. The mean family size of 5.1 children for completed first marriages was notably small; but by itself this tells us little, since the low mean may have been the result either of family limitation or of such factors as sex selection, infant mortality, and low fecundity. Some light is thrown on the subject, however, by the distribution of completed families by size.

As Figure 5.3 shows, there was a heavy bunching around the mean, with few completed families having less than four or more

[1] When families where a child had died are excluded from the pool of families with three or more children, the proportion of males in the next registered birth changed from 0.42 to 0.40 in the *PM* group, and from 0.63 to 0.68 in the *PF* group. There was no change in the *M = F* group, where the proportion remained at 0.63.

than seven children. The extreme bunching of this distribution can be brought out by a comparison of Nakahara with Meulan in France, using only completed marriages that began at the wife's age 30 or less.[9] Only 10 percent of completed families in Nakahara had eight or more children, compared with 57 percent in Meulan during a period of no family limitation (1660–1739); and only 8 percent of completed families in Nakahara had two or fewer children, compared with 33 percent in Meulan during a period of family limitation (1790–1839).[10]

Still more remarkable is the rarity of small families and the complete absence of childless families in Nakahara. Since such families, if desired, could have been achieved through abortion or infanticide, their rarity must have been intentional. The avoidance of childless families is especially clear. About 4 percent of any human population may be expected to be sterile, and merely letting matters take their course would almost certainly have produced some childless families. But matters were not allowed to take their course: infertile brides were sent home early, as is evident from the fact that 10 of 13 divorces in the village ended childless marriages after an average 3.0 years of conjugal living. In other words, childless marriages never became completed marriages.

It is not immediately obvious that the rarity of large families was in any way intentional, since the death of children from natural causes prior to registration would tend to produce this result. But

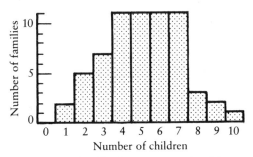

Fig. 5.3. Distribution by completed family size, 64 completed first marriages. The absence of childless families is explained by the tendency of husbands to divorce barren brides; see pp. 102–3 for more on this point.

there is some hint of intention in this regard, too, in the evidence concerning the mean age of mothers at the birth of the last child (*MALB*), which for obvious reasons is a meaningful datum only when marriages are completed. The mean *MALB* in completed first marriages in Nakahara was 37.5—rather early for a population not practicing family limitation.[j] But the early *MALB* may be accounted for by infants dying, unregistered, of natural causes after the last registered birth. Also, the early age of marriage for females might have enabled subfecund couples, who could well have been childless in a late-marrying population, to have one or two children at an early age.

However, if we divide the mothers into two nearly equal groups, early stoppers (*MALB* 37.0 or less) and late stoppers (*MALB* over 37.0), we almost rule out these possibilities for the critical early group. The total of last births to early stoppers, whose mean *MALB* was 33.0 as compared with 41.2 for late stoppers, contained 21 male children and 8 females, a topheavy sex ratio of 262. Late stoppers, with 19 males and 16 females as last births, had a ratio of only 119. Thus much of the early stopping was apparently deliberate. If it had been involuntary (for example, the result of infecundity or "infant mortality"), the sex of the last child would have been randomly determined and not skewed heavily in favor of males.

Significantly, though not surprisingly, early stoppers had fewer children than late. The mean completed family size of the two groups, respectively, was 4.0 and 6.1; and although only 10 percent of early stoppers had as many as six children, an astonishing 71 percent of late stoppers did. The difference is not attributable to a difference in years of marriage, since the average duration of marriage for the two groups of women was nearly identical (19.4 years and 19.6 years), and since all members of both groups remained married through age 45. The smaller families, therefore, were evidently due mainly to early stopping, a good deal of which must have been deliberate to account for the heavy predominance of males as last children.

---

[j]In eighteenth-century European communities practicing little or no family limitation, the mean *MALB* was about 40 or 41.

This leaves open the possibility that late stoppers did not practice infanticide. After all, they stopped with one sex about as often as the other and bore as many females as males (exactly 106 of each). Abstention from infanticide would also account for the late *MALB* that characterized the group. But late stoppers were not in fact abstainers. This appears when the group is subdivided into *PM*, *M = F*, and *PF* groups, as all families were earlier, on the basis of the sex of two or more children registered at home, and the sex of the next child observed for each group. As Table 5.3 shows, the probability of a male birth increased by large jumps from *PM* to *M = F* to *PF* families.[11]

It would therefore appear that late stoppers continued child-bearing to a relatively late age *despite* the practice of infanticide; that by infanticide they tended to keep offspring sexually balanced from one birth to another after the second child (though in doing so, judging from the sex ratio, they apparently did not "return" as many infants as the early stoppers); and that the large size of completed families among them would not generally have been due to a need to continue procreation to a late age in order to correct a severe sex imbalance among early children. Assuming these conclusions are warranted, we may add another: both sex balance and

TABLE 5.3
Sex of Next Child Relative to Sibling Sets,
MALB Groups in Complete First Marriages

MALB group and sibling category	Sex of next child		Sex ratio
	Males	Females	
Early stoppers			
PM	9	11	82
M = F	12	4	300
PF	15	3	500
Late stoppers			
PM	21	34	62
M = F	19	17	112
PF	23	16	144

NOTE: Includes only families with two or more living siblings at time of next birth. *MALB* of early group is 37 or less; that of late group is over 37.

larger-than-average family size were in all probability intentional, and late stopping was the necessary means of achieving these goals.

Farm Size and Family Size

We come now to another kind of evidence for family limitation. Although there is no direct information on farm size, we have a reasonable proxy in the MC estimates of the normal productivity of holdings in rice equivalents (*kokudaka*) for all holdings in the village, identified by holder, at ten scattered dates (see Chapter 3). The accuracy and currency of these evaluations, which were made for purposes of taxation, are uncertain; also, they tell us nothing about how land was distributed for farming as opposed to how it was held for purposes of taxation (roughly, ownership); nor do they reveal anything about the nonagricultural income of families. Nevertheless, we have found these data relevant in analyzing mortality in Nakahara (see pp. 51–52). We use them here to divide all completed first marriages into families above and below the median holding, or large and small holders.[12] There were 32 Nakahara families in each category.

Completed family size was significantly different for the two groups: large holders had an average of 5.7 children, small 4.5. This was because large holders' wives married at an average age of 18.5 years (as opposed to the small holders' 20.5) but had their last birth at age 37.9 (small holders were 36.1); thus the wives of large holders had a childbearing period nearly four years longer. But size of holding did not affect the spacing of children. If we divide the mean number of children by the difference between mean MALB and mean wife's age at marriage, we get 0.29 children per year in each group.

It is interesting that both large and small holders break down almost evenly into early and late stoppers, and that size of holding and MALB together determine family size to a greater degree than either alone. This can be seen in Figure 5.4, where we divide completed families into four groups based on a combination of holding size and MALB. We arrange the four groups down the page in descending order of average family size and show for each group the

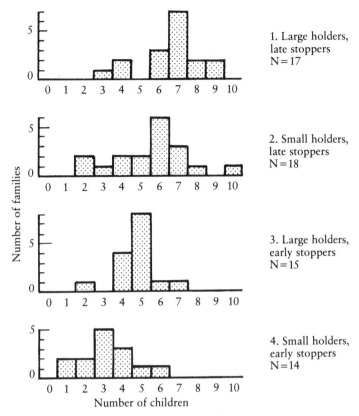

Fig. 5.4. Distribution by completed family size, 64 completed first marriages grouped by landholding and mother's age at last birth

distribution of families by size. Notice that the order turns out to be alternately large and small holders. Each group has a very strongly marked or modal family size that accounts for one-third to more than half the families in it, and the mode decreases neatly as we move down the page. Moreover, smallest family size and largest family size for the various groups also decrease in the same order, though a bit less smoothly. These groups defined by holding size and *MALB*, thus seem to have quite distinct fertility characteristics.

Average family size is clearly related to holding size. Early-stopping large holders had larger families than early-stopping small holders, and late-stopping large holders had larger families than late-stopping small holders. This would seem to be because large holders wanted more children, since they could better afford them and could use the additional labor more efficiently in farming. In any case, holding size was not the only determinant of family size; late or early stopping, which was independent of holding size, was equally or almost equally important. This can be seen in the fact that late-stopping small holders had more children than early-stopping large holders, though whether accidentally or intentionally we cannot guess.

Sex Selection and Family Size

Besides aiming at a particular number of children, a Nakahara family would usually have wanted a particular sex mix and birth sequence. These objectives obviously must have gotten in the way of one another. Accepting or "returning" children because of the sex of the infant would tend to defeat plans about completed family size, and vice versa. It is surprising, therefore, that a clear relation emerges between completed family size and the sex ratio of children. The larger the family, generally speaking, the more evenly balanced the sexes; the smaller the family, the higher the proportion of boys. We must qualify this statement before exploring possible explanations of what it says.

Families of the smallest size used in testing the relationship—one to three children—were in fact almost evenly divided between boys and girls. But if we divide this group into early and late stoppers, we find that the ten early stoppers had a total of fifteen boys and eight girls, at a mean interval of 3.8 years; however, the four late stoppers had only two boys to eight girls (interval 6.1 years). This difference may be due to sampling error, since the number in each group is small. But another explanation is also possible. Late stoppers with three children or fewer had long intervals between births; this raises the suspicion that they may have tried repeatedly for males, failed to get them, and after annulling a number of births finally settled for females. If so, the early stoppers, who were much the more numerous group, would more accurately reflect the intentions of small families.

With the qualification, then, that a few small families ended up unintentionally with a high proportion of girls, the statement holds that the ratio of male to female children was high in small completed families, and converged to normal as family size increased. Omitting the possibly anomalous group of late stoppers among the smallest families, we find the following progression:

Family size	M	F	Sex ratio
1–3 (small)	15	8	188
4–5 (medium)	56	43	130
6 or more (large)	101	94	107

One naturally wonders to what extent the relation between family size and sex ratio was the outcome of different family strategies, and to what extent it was due to factors beyond anyone's control. It will be obvious to the wary reader that we cannot really hope to answer this question, but some observations leading toward an answer may be possible.

Three partial explanations hinging on unintentional factors can probably be rejected. One turns on the wife's age at first marriage. The earlier that age, the larger the mean completed family size tended to be: in 33 completed families where the wives married at age 18 or less, the mean was 5.7 children; 22 marriages at ages 19 to 21 had a mean of 4.7; and in the nine marriages at age 22 or older, the mean was 3.8. Now, *if* couples also tended first to have a certain number of males and then accepted females in the event they had more children, *then* the earlier the marriage the larger the completed family would be, and the lower the sex ratio of the children. But this does not seem to have been the case in fact. Women married before age 22 in 86 percent of all complete first marriages, and the mean age of marriage for women with four or five children and women bearing six or more was nearly identical:

Family size	No. of families	Mean age of marriage	Mean MALB
1–3 (small)	14	22.9	33.4
4–5 (medium)	22	18.7	36.0
6 or more (large)	28	18.4	40.8

Age of marriage, then, would seem to have had no influence on family size *after* three children, and hence none on the difference in sex ratio between the two larger categories of family size.

Another possible explanation concerns the effects of mortality on completed family size. Inasmuch as large families had proportionately more deaths among their children before the birth of the last child than small families,[k] the desire to replace lost children may have prompted some families to continue procreation longer than they would have otherwise, and also to accept more female births. On the other hand, they may have suffered more deaths before the birth of the last child merely because childbearing continued longer. tinued longer.

If we count the proportion of children born and dying before the mother's age 38, the figure is 7 percent in small families, 13 percent in medium families, and 14 percent in large families. Although there may be a real difference between very small families and the others, there is none among families with more than three children. Furthermore, if we eliminate deceased children in computing mean family size, we still find a significant difference between the groups: a 2.4-child mean in the smallest families, 4.1 in the medium-sized, and 5.9 in the large. Thus child replacement would seem to account only marginally, at best, for the difference in completed family size and sex ratio.

The third explanation has already been rejected in another connection. The suggestion there was: although small families practiced infanticide in favor of males, large families rarely resorted to infanticide, and so ended up inadvertently with approximately the same number of males as females. This line of reasoning, however, does not square with the facts. If we consider only the group of largest families (six-plus children) and classify the births of their children in relation to the sex balance of existing children (two or more), as we did earlier, the next children born were divided by sex as follows:

Existing children	M	F	Sex ratio
PM	22	36	61
M = F	19	13	146
PF	23	14	164

[k] For completed first marriages, the proportion of children who died before the birth of the last child was 17 percent in families of 6 or more children, 12 percent in families of 4–5 children, and 11 percent in families of 1–3 children.

The probability of the next child being female rises from 0.38 for *PF* families to 0.41 for *M = F*, and to 0.62 for *PM*. This suggests that large families were intentionally large and intentionally sex-balanced.

The Relation Between Family Size and the Sex of Children

To say that the connection between family size and the sex of children was in some degree intentional is far from specifying the nature of the intention, about which we can only speculate. Our guess is that all families wanted at a minimum one or two male children, who could provide valuable labor and also became heirs to the family headship. Small families were predominantly male, therefore, because they accepted male children, tended to eliminate females, and stopped procreation early. But few families wanted many more than the minimum number of males, for fear of causing future competition for the family headship and creating either pressure to divide property or problems in providing for noninheriting sons. After a few sons had been born, female children were as desirable as males—or more so, since they raised none of these problems and could perform tasks in the house and on the farm that were unsuitable for males. They were also valuable as a means of affiliation with other families; and they could inherit if the male line gave out, or could help recruit an adoptive heir through marriage.

The more children a family had, then, the higher the proportion of girls was likely to be. This is not meant to imply that large families first assured themselves of the minimum number of males and then added females in later births. We already have reason to believe that this was not the case; on the contrary, large families tended to keep the sexes in balance as they went along, which suggests an approximate goal for ultimate family size that was pursued from the start.

The Spacing of Children

If we may cautiously conclude that infanticide sometimes enabled families to approximate the number and sex of the children they wanted, we must then ask whether it was also of help in spacing children conveniently. Table 5.4 shows, for completed first mar-

TABLE 5.4
*Registered Birth Intervals in Completed
First Marriages*

Birth interval	Number	Mean (year)	Standard deviation (year)
0–1	64	2.6	2.3
1–2	57	4.4	2.3
2–3	50	3.3	1.5
3–4	39	3.2	0.9
4–5	28	3.5	1.8
Penultimate	57	3.9	1.9
Ultimate	62	4.2	2.4

NOTE: First-birth intervals are not counted as penultimate or last-birth intervals; and any interval for birth orders 2–5 that also happened to be the last birth for the mother is counted in the tabulation for only the ultimate birth interval.

riages, the mean registered birth interval, in years and fractions of years, for intervals 0–1 (marriage to first child) to 4–5, and also for the penultimate and ultimate intervals.[13] If we keep in mind comparable data from European parishes, three features of the table stand out. First, the intervals tended to be very long; second, after the 1–2 interval they showed no decided tendency to lengthen until the last interval; and third, the 1–2 interval is much longer than subsequent intervals, whereas in European parishes it invariably seems to be shorter.[1]

The length and uniformity of the Nakahara intervals (after the first two) would seem to result from the unregistered births in our data, which would include infanticide for purposes of family limitation and sex selection, independently of considerations of spacing. This is suggested by the fact that at almost every interval the distribution of cases ranges from short to extremely long, with no pronounced mode. If families were spacing for convenience, their standards of convenience were too various to be perceptible.

But the 1–2 interval may be an exception. Its length is so idiosyn-

[1]For example, for completed marriages between 1740 and 1789 in Meulan, France, the mean second-birth interval is 1.5 years, as compared with 1.7 years for the third-birth interval, 1.8 years for the fourth-birth interval, and 2.1 years for the fifth-birth interval. See Lachiver, *Meulan*, p. 184.

cratic and yet so consistent, standing out clearly in every subset of families, that one suspects a deliberate prolongation of this interval by some families. We chose to speculate that the second child might have differed from all others in ways that affected timing, as follows. The first child had to come as soon as possible after marriage to prove the fertility of the bride. Beginning with the third child, given average spacing, there would be one or more older children in the house to care for the new arrival. Thus, the first child would be age 7 at the birth of the third child and in many ways able to care for himself and help with the baby. At later births the existing children would be still older, and the mother's situation still easier. But with normal spacing the first child would be only 4.4 at the second birth—that is, unable to care for himself, let alone help with another child. And this would have come at a time when, through the decease or aging of the husband's parents, the mother's responsibilities in the house and on the farm were becoming heavier. She and her husband might consequently be tempted to defer the second birth until the first child was somewhat older. The deferral would be less likely, however, if the husband's mother were still alive, if an unmarried sister were at home, or if there were some other adult female in the house.

We therefore divided all completed first marriages into families in which another adult female was present at the time of the second birth and those in which there was none, excluding families in which the first child died or departed before the birth of the second. The mean 1–2 interval was significantly different ($p < 0.05$) in the two groups—3.5 and 5.1 years, respectively.[m] Only 18 percent of the birth intervals in the first group were five years or more and only 5 percent were seven years or more, whereas the corresponding percentages for the second group were 47 percent and 28 percent. One suspects, therefore, some deliberate spacing for the convenience of the mother at the second birth (and possibly also at other births, for reasons that we are unable to discern).

[m] The numbers of families in these groups were 22 and 32, respectively. A test of the difference in means yields a t statistic of 2.3, significant at the 0.05 level on 52 degrees of freedom.

Shape of the Fertility Curve

The data on spacing bring us back, briefly, to a point mentioned earlier: age-specific fertility in Nakahara shows a convex curve of the kind usually associated with unrestricted births, not the concave curve associated with birth control. The reasons for the shape of the curve in Nakahara, where births were limited by infanticide, can now be seen to be the following. First, infanticide gave rise to a pattern of births different from one that would accompany other forms of limitation because it is a sex-selective process: some children of an unwanted sex were eliminated at every birth order in the population, creating exceptionally long average intervals between registered births. Second, the smaller the completed family, the more sex selection was likely to have taken place, and the longer the mean interval between births was likely to be. Families of three or fewer children had a mean of 4.4 years; families with four or five and those with six or more averaged 3.8 and 3.2 years, respectively. Finally, Nakaharans had fewer very small and childless families, as already noted, than populations limiting births generally have.

The combined result of these three factors was to spread childbearing out over the fertile years of marriage, instead of concentrating it in the early years; hence the major factor in difference in fertility between one age group and another was declining fecundity as aging produced an increasing proportion of infertile women, which tends to give a convex curve.

If infanticide had been practiced without sex selection, presumably it would not have been used until females had reached the desired size, and would then have been vigorously enforced. This would make the average birth interval relatively short and would give fertility a concave curve. But it seems most unlikely that any population would accept infanticide as a normal means of family limitation without also using it to control the sex composition of sibling sets.

Conclusions

Infanticide, common in the past in both Asia and the West, has been seen by historians mainly as a product of social demoralization and the struggle of parents to keep themselves and their favored progeny alive.[14] This may be justified generally, though it is obviously a view based mainly on literary and legal evidence with a strong moral and class bias. But it fits the Nakahara case badly. Infanticide seems to have been widely practiced there by what might be thought to be the most respectable and stable part of the population: married couples who, at a time when divorce and early death were common, lived together through the wives' fecund years, a term completed by only 59 percent of first-married couples. Also, infanticide seems to have been practiced by large holders as well as small, and by all holders as often in good as in bad crop years. At any rate, we find no difference in registered births per thousand population in years when rice was dear and when it was cheap (see Table 5.5), though the marriage rate differs significantly for these groups of years.[n]

Among the apparent objectives of infanticide in Nakahara were: overall family limitation; an equilibrium of some sort between family size and farm size; an advantageous distribution of the sexes in children; possibly the spacing of children in a way convenient to the mother; and the avoidance of a particular sex in the next child. These goals required foresight and the ability to carry out long-range plans, qualities not usually associated with demoralized or desperate people. What proportion of families used infanticide to realize some or all of these goals, which tended to overlap, we cannot say. Given the degree of agreement on completed family size in particular subgroups, the percentage may have been substantial.

Most important, we do not know how common in Tokugawa society this pattern of infanticide was. It cannot be emphasized too strongly that Nakahara was a village with a population that never exceeded 300, one of thousands that size, and possibly highly deviant. No general significance can be attributed to our findings until, in some respects at least, they have been duplicated elsewhere.

[n] Prices used here are spring and fall rice prices for the Mitsui main store in Kyoto, over a hundred kilometers away. See Mitsui bunkō, pp. 67ff. Prices and demographic events were not matched by chronological years, but were offset to take account of the normal lag between an occurrence and its recording at the end of the registration year, as well as the six-month overlap between registration year and calendar year.

TABLE 5.5
Prices, Births, and Marriages

Price years	Births per 1,000 person-years	Marriages per 1,000 person-years*
Upper third	29.1	33.7
Middle third	26.7	46.7
Lower third	27.4	60.1

*Population base taken to be unmarried adults, ages 15–45 only.

Indeed, at a time when even the design of spades and mattocks differed from one village to the next, it would be folly to expect in villages practicing infanticide that the patterns of family limitation and sex selection would be everywhere closely similar. It does not seem improbable, for example, that some villages discriminated overall against males in about the same degree that Nakahara discriminated overall against females. Nor is it unlikely that the sex bias changed from one period to another in the same village; or that different strata in the same village discriminated against different sexes, or against the same sex in significantly different degree. It will be important in looking for patterns, therefore, to disaggregate data as much as possible in order to prevent contrary tendencies from canceling one another and producing an overall appearance of normality.

If such differences may be reasonably expected within and between villages, we should not expect continuity from one region, historical background, ecology, or economic structure to others. If variety on the basis of these variables was as great as we believe, assuming infanticide to have been widespread, it will take a great amount of ingenuity and patience to uncover it; and at every stage efforts will be hampered by the small size of villages. But if in time systematic differences do appear, we may begin to be able to identify various kinds of reproductive behavior and their social correlates in preindustrial Japan, and possibly to fashion a test of some general use in distinguishing types of groups and communities.

No amount of research in population registers, however, is likely to answer the question of motivation raised by the Nakahara materials. We could understand infanticide if it had been a function of poverty—a form of self-preservation—as we believed at the beginning, but it was not wholly, or perhaps even mainly, that. In important degree it seems to have been a kind of family planning with long-range objectives. One is bound to wonder about the nature of the objectives of planning, and how they were symbolized and phrased so that infanticide could become (apparently) a normal, even conventional, form of behavior.

Chapter Six   Nuptiality

B<small>Y NUPTIALITY</small> we mean (1) the proportion of the population who never marry, which in practice is taken to be those persons not married by age 50, and (2) the distribution of others of each sex by age at first marriage. Both these aspects of nuptiality have a powerful effect on fertility.

Two general patterns of nuptiality have been found in preindustrial societies: the "non-European" pattern of early and nearly universal marriage, and the pattern of late marriage and frequent celibacy[a] that came to prevail over most of Western Europe about the sixteenth century and, so far as is known, has not occurred elsewhere. For our purposes, the European pattern may be defined more exactly as a mean age at first marriage of 25 or more for women and a proportion of 10 percent or more never married by age 50. By contrast, the mean age at first marriage in non-European populations is usually under 20 for women (though often higher for men), with a proportion of less than 5 percent never marrying.

The European pattern is associated with lower general fertility, since women are married during significantly fewer fecund years—in some cases 50 percent fewer—and since a considerable number of women never marry. However, for reasons not well understood the European pattern tends to be linked with distinctly higher age-

---

[a] We use the word "celibacy" throughout this chapter to mean abstention not from sexual relations but from marriage. Celibacy at a given age, say 30, therefore means unmarried up to age 30. "Definitive celibacy" means celibate at age 50, even though the person may subsequently marry. After 50 marriage is rare, and reproduction for women highly unlikely.

specific fertility in marriage. Perhaps marital fertility in non-European populations is held down more severely by suckling practices, taboos on sexual relations at certain periods, and dietary deficiencies. It is almost as if some populations consciously or unconsciously restricted fertility in marriage and others restricted marriage itself. The second would be the more effective check on fertility, though both systems hold it well below the physiological maximum.

We already know that marital fertility in Nakahara was extremely low by eighteenth-century European standards. Was marriage accordingly early and nearly universal, and if so, did marriage practices in Nakahara serve to limit fertility in no important way? Before turning to these questions, however, we must briefly discuss certain problems of estimating mean age at first marriage and the proportions married at various ages.

Age at First Marriage

Three features of the basic Tokugawa population register (*SAC*) tend to give an upward bias to estimates of age at first marriage. One is the existence of gap years—i.e. years of no record—which occur in nearly all long series of registers. Although gaps have little or no effect on the computation of many demographic rates, they may seriously affect measures such as mean interval between births or mean age at first marriage, which depend on the continuous observation of individuals or couples. Thus a marriage may be missed because it occurs and is dissolved in a gap, and the later remarriage of one of the parties may be mistaken for a first marriage. Such cases, of course, will spuriously raise the mean age at first marriage, and the longer and the more frequent the gaps in the record, the greater the chance of serious overestimation.[b]

The basic *SAC* series in Nakahara contained a number of long gaps (see Chapter 2); fortunately, we were able to recover vital events for nearly all the years from the supplementary *ZGC* regis-

---

[b] There is also a problem in dating marriages in a gap. But this can be handled in the same way as the dating of deaths in a gap: either by dating at the midway point or by assigning dates randomly.

ter. Only in the 13 widely spaced gap years that remain would we miss a marriage, and then only if the marriage occurred and was dissolved in the gap. Since gaps are few and short—two gaps of three years and seven of one year each—missed marriages are certainly few and may be nil.[c]

A second source of possible bias is that we have no reliable way of knowing whether marriage partners coming into Nakahara from outside, usually brides, were marrying for the first or a later time (see Table 6.1). One automatically eliminates from the group any bride (or groom) accompanied by children. But this is not a really trustworthy indicator of second marriage, since widows and divorcées without children were more likely to remarry than those with children (see pp. 100–103). Brides entering from outside are therefore likely to include an unknown number of second or later marriages, and it is important to keep them separate from brides born and raised in the village, whose order of marriage is reliably known. It turns out that in Nakahara the mean age at first marriage for the two groups was not significantly different; but this could not have been inferred in advance and may not have been the case in other villages.

A third source of possible bias is the late registration of marriages. According to the Meiji compilation on Tokugawa customary law, the timing of registration varied greatly from place to place: in some districts it occurred at the time of the wedding or within a few days, whereas in others registration was delayed for some years or until the bride proved satisfactory to the groom's family.[d] There is no evidence of delayed registration in Nakahara, however. We

[c] It should also be remembered that omissions would be innocuous unless (1) the missing cases represent a different age pattern of first marriage from other marriages, or (2) at least one party to missed marriages later remarried, so that the second marriage was mistaken for a first.

[d] In Kawachi Province, Sara District, "The marriage is not reported in writing. Usually on the following day or on the second day after the wedding ceremony, the marriage is reported orally to the headman and elders." In Izu Province, Tagata District, "The transfer of family status is made only when the bride has proved fitting to the family." In Awa Province, "A marriage is usually not registered until a child is born." See Wigmore, *Law and Justice*, VII, 44–46.

TABLE 6.1
Nakahara Marriages by Origin of Spouse and Order of Marriage

| | Husband's origin | | | |
Wife's origin	In-village, 1st marriage	In-village, 2d or later marriage	Out-village	Total
In-village, 1st marriage	21(12)*	1(1)	5(3)	27(15)
In-village, 2d or later marriage	3(2)	2(1)	4(2)	9(5)
Out-village, with children	3(2)	0	0	3(2)
Out-village, without children	128(71)	10(6)	1(1)	139(78)
TOTAL	155(87)	13(7)	10(6)	178(100)

* Figures in parentheses are percentages of all marriages.

found only three registered cases of brides with children, and surprisingly few of children registered as born in the first year of marriage (only 3 of the 64 first births in complete first marriages). Cases
of both kinds should have been frequent if registration were delayed
very often. But wherever delayed registration was common, it
would give a strong upward bias to age at first marriage, since marriages would actually begin an unknown time before registration,
and a certain proportion of "trial marriages" would end without
record.

Calculation of Probability of Marriage or Celibacy

Some data used by demographers do not allow one to distinguish
persons who have never been married from those who have been
divorced or have lost spouses through death. We do not have this
problem in Nakahara. Except for occasional servants from outside
and a few families of immigrants—all of whom we omitted in calculating proportions marrying—everyone in our register was either
born or reared in the village or entered it for marriage. We have no
trouble, therefore, in calculating for this population the proportion
of each sex who reached age 50 without marrying. But a moment's
reflection will show that this is not a very useful figure, since it takes

no account of the effects of migration and mortality, which are likely to have been great in a small population.

Since the probability of a single person marrying before 50 obviously depends heavily on his or her age, the age pattern of death and migration will profoundly affect the proportion who remain celibate at age 50. Louis Henry has suggested a technique, used here, for calculating the probability of celibacy at various ages while controlling for migration and mortality. It is based on the somewhat unrealistic assumption that people who die or migrate single at any given age have the same chance of marrying as people of the same sex who do neither. In effect, this tells us what the proportion of celibacy at various ages would be in the complete absence of migration and death. We call this figure the probability of celibacy. In Nakahara, it almost certainly overestimates the male marriage rate, since male migrants left the village in most cases because they were not heirs and therefore probably had a lesser chance of marriage than those who stayed at home. But any other assumption would be equally arbitrary. (Tables 6.2 and 6.4 show calculations of the *probability* that males and females, respectively, who have never married by age x will remain unmarried during the next five years.)

Males

The probability of any given male marrying inside Nakahara was strongly influenced by inheritance. Nearly all males marrying for the first time in the village either were at the time or later became family heads:

	N	Percent
Family head at time of marriage or subsequently	106	65
Founded branch family	45	28
Never family head	9	6
Unknown owing to end of record	3	2

It does not follow that all males who became family heads married: in fact, 16 of 123 who succeeded to headship failed to marry, though in most cases this was because of early death, and another eight were unmarried at the end of the record in 1830.

Sons who did not become family heads typically either left Nakahara, in which case we usually know nothing of their ultimate matrimonial fate, or remained unmarried in the village. Those who stayed, together with a few celibate family heads, give Nakahara a moderately high male celibacy rate. Fifteen, or 12 percent, of the 128 males who reached age 50 in the village did not marry by that age (or later, as it happens). If we use Henry's method to take into account the experience of all males born in Nakahara, including those who died or migrated single before 50, we can compute the probability of celibacy at various ages separately for small, medium, and large holding families, that is, lower, middle, and upper classes (see Table 6.2).

The tendency to late marriage and large class differences in this respect are the two most striking features of the results. The proportion of all males who were likely to be still single did not drop below half until almost age 30. The reason for such late marriages was undoubtedly the close link between marriage and family headship. We have already seen that most males who married also became family heads, and the timing of the marriage in a high proportion of cases was just before or after succession to that position.[e] The reasons for this must wait until a later chapter for explanation. Here, it will be enough to say that the addition of a bride often required radical changes in the family, including the departure of the groom's brothers and sisters; and families tended to postpone this dangerous reorganization of the labor force until the actual or impending succession of a new heir made it necessary.

The probability of celibacy at the higher ages varied greatly by class, but when we turn to mean age at first marriage class differences seem to narrow considerably. There was a difference of only 1.5 years between the lower and upper classes (Table 6.3). Class differences emerged sharply again, however, in the overall distribution of marriage ages. Clearly there were obstacles to male marriage in poor families that were not present or were less formi-

[e] Some 27 percent of family heads who married did so in the year of succession to the family headship or in the year just before or after; 55 percent married within four years before or after, and 73 percent within seven years before or after.

TABLE 6.2
Probability of Male Celibacy by Age
and Economic Class

(Males born in Nakahara, 1707–80)

| Age | Economic class* | | | |
	Lower	Middle	Upper	All
20	.94	.93	.93	.93
25	.88	.65	.67	.72
30	.67	.29	.38	.42
35	.41	.20	.20	.25
40	.41	.10	.04	.14
45	.41	.10	.04	.14
50	.28	.10	.04	.12

* Lower-class holdings were 0–4 koku; middle-class, 4.1–18.0; upper-class, over 18.0.

TABLE 6.3
Nakahara Marriages by Husband's Age at First Marriage
and Economic Class

(Males born in Nakahara after 1716, married before 1831)

| Husband's age at marriage | N | Husband's economic class | | | |
		Lower (N = 20)	Middle (N = 37)	Upper (N = 37)	All (N = 94)
15–19	4	0%	3%	8%	4%
20–24	34	35	41	32	36
25–29	32	25	38	35	34
30–34	15	25	11	16	16
35 or more	9	15	8	8	10
Mean		28.2 yr.	26.9 yr.	26.7 yr.	27.1 yr.
Median		27.5	26.5	26.5	26.5

dable in richer families. Among the possibilities that come to mind are the proportionately greater burden of an additional member in a poor family, the greater relative cost of marriage festivities, and the greater difficulty of attracting a bride. We will encounter some evidence of these factors in a later chapter.

Females

In contrast to males, females born and reared in Nakahara married early and almost universally. With them, we do not have the problem of a subject leaving the village single and never returning. A few single women of marriageable age disappeared permanently from the record in gap years, but probably all had either died or married out of the village; in calculating the proportion of women marrying at various ages, however, we treated these disappearances as if they were deaths. In only one case did a single woman leave the village permanently while under observation. There were many cases of temporary female migration for work, usually for only a year or two, and after returning to Nakahara these women almost invariably married. In fact, only three Nakahara women of any description who reached age 32 in the register failed to marry sooner or later.

Calculating by Henry's method the probability of Nakahara females being single at various ages gives the results seen in Table 6.4. Again we see significant class differences. A large majority of upper-class women were likely to be married by 20, as compared to about half of the middle class and only one in five of the lower class. The probability of a woman remaining single as late as age 25 was three to six times greater in the lower class than in the other two classes; but from age 30 on there was not much difference.

Table 6.5 shows the mean and median ages and the distribution of ages at first marriage for women native to Nakahara. The overall mean and median, 19.9 and 18.5 years, clearly belong to the non-European marriage pattern, and class differences are much more pronounced than among men. The reason for this may be that male marriage was postponed as long as possible for reasons that were similar in all families, whereas the female age of marriage depended to a considerable extent on family size, which varied by economic stratum (see Chapter 8). In any case, whereas the difference in mean age at first marriage between lower and upper classes was 1.5 years for males, it was 5.0 for females.

No doubt the richer the family the more desirable the daughter generally was as a bride, and this may have had something to do with class differences in female marriage age. But the more important reason was probably the greater value of a woman to her own family when the family was poor, and the consequent reluc-

TABLE 6.4
Probability of Female Celibacy by Age and Economic Class
(Females born in Nakahara, 1707–80)

Age	Economic class			All
	Lower	Middle	Upper	
15	1.00	.95	.90	.94
20	.83	.56	.29	.50
25	.64	.19	.10	.26
30	.18	.08	.06	.09
35	.09	0	.06	.04
40	.09	0	.06	.04
45	.09	0	.06	.04
50	.09	0	.06	.04

TABLE 6.5
*Nakahara Marriages by Wife's Age at First Marriage
and Economic Class*
(Females born in Nakahara after 1716, married before 1831)

Wife's age at marriage	N	Wife's economic class			All (N = 151)
		Lower (N = 42)	Middle (N = 48)	Upper (N = 61)	
14 or less	16	5%	10%	15%	11%
15–19	74	31	46	64	49
20–24	38	31	27	20	25
25–29	16	24	10	2	11
30–34	6	7	6	0	4
35–39	1	2	0	0	1
Mean		22.6 yr.	20.4 yr.	17.6 yr.	19.6 yr.
Median		22.5	19.5	17.5	18.5

tance of the family to give her up as a bride. There is a strong hint of this in Hayami's finding in a neighboring village that girls who worked out as servants before marriage married on average 3.4 years later than girls who did not, and that girls with premarital work-out experience were more numerous in poor than in well-to-do families.[1] This was also the case in Nakahara. Of girls born after 1716 and marrying before 1831, 24 percent from lower-class and 19 percent from middle-class but only 5 percent from upper-class families were employed before marriage. Poor families evidently delayed the marriage of daughters longer than other families in order to benefit from the girls' earnings in the meantime.

But this was by no means the whole story. For if we eliminate brides who had previously worked as servants, the mean age of first marriage becomes 21.3 for lower-class, 20.1 for middle-class, and 17.6 for upper-class women. That is, the spread narrows but remains significant. The residual difference would seem to reflect the differential value of the women *at home*. This can hardly be because the total labor demand was greater on small holdings than on large. However, family size varied directly and significantly with holding size (as will be seen in later chapters), and the smaller the family, the more critical the role of the daughter was likely to be. In a small family she might well be the only adult female and consequently not only a part-time field hand but also cook, housekeeper, and surrogate mother to young children.

This inference is strengthened when all families are sorted into three approximately equal groups determined by family size in the year before marrying out a daughter. We then see that the smaller the family, the later the girl tended to marry, regardless of economic class. Also, the spread in mean age of first marriage for daughters between the largest families (7–10 members) and the smallest (2–3 members) was approximately as great as that between large and small holders (see pp. 144–45). What determined whether a girl was released early or late for marriage was evidently in large part her marginal value at home.

Brides from Outside

So far we have been considering women native to Nakahara, whose careers can be followed almost continuously from birth—a group in which the danger of mistaking order of marriage is slight. This is not the case with brides from outside, and we must assume among them an unknown number of women who were marrying for the second time or third time. But the mean and median ages of marriage in this group—20.4 and 18.5—are also quite low, strongly confirming the pattern of early marriage found among Nakahara women (see Table 6.6).

TABLE 6.6

Marriages Between Nakahara Men and Outsiders by Wife's Age
at Marriage and Husband's Economic Class

(Females marrying into Nakahara, 1717–1830)

Wife's age at marriage	N	Husband's economic class			All (N = 139)
		Lower (N = 37)	Middle (N = 56)	Upper (N = 46)	
14 or less	6	0%	4%	9%	4%
15–19	85	32	64	80	61
20–24	25	32	20	4	18
25–29	14	22	7	4	10
30–34	5	11	2	0	4
35 or more	4	3	4	2	3
Mean		23.6 yr.	20.2 yr.	18.0 yr.	20.4 yr.
Median		22.5	18.5	17.5	18.5

When incoming brides are classified by the economic status of the families they married into, we find the same class differences as those for Nakahara women when classified by natal family. Brides entering lower-class families averaged 3.4 years older than those entering the middle class and 5.6 years older than those entering the upper class. Clearly, these differences cannot be explained by any differential value of female labor in the receiving families, which might explain the timing of the marriage but not the age of the bride. The only plausible explanation would seem to be that brides tended to marry into families of approximately the same class as their own.[f]

Age Difference Between Spouses

Given the linkage of male marriage to inheritance, it is easy to understand why men married in their late twenties. But it is not

---

[f]It is impossible to test this inference directly for a satisfactory number of cases by matching the status of families linked by marriage, since families tended to marry across village boundaries. But the 23 marriages between Nakahara families are nonetheless suggestive. Eleven of these were between families of the same class; in seven the bride's family was lower in status than the groom's; and in five it was higher. Lateral marriages do seem somewhat overrepresented, but the total number of cases is too small to know what significance to attach to this.

obvious why women married young; or rather, why there was a spread of 7.2 years in mean age between spouses at first marriage. Grooms no doubt preferred girls in their teens to women in their middle or late twenties, but this cannot be the whole explanation. The same preference must have been present in eighteenth-century Europe; yet European men, who married at about the same average age as men in Nakahara, tended to marry women near their own age, and frequently married older women.

The explanation may lie in the institution of dowry. Dowry was a major form of inheritance in Europe, representing a substantial transfer of property from one family to another. A bride's parents therefore had a strong incentive to postpone the transfer as long as possible, in order to use the property longer. Girls with a good dowry would usually not be available as brides before their middle or late twenties, and if a man insisted on marrying a younger woman, he would normally have to forgo a dowry. This would be a violation of ordinary prudence if he was setting up an independent household; and if he was also hoping to inherit from still-living parents, prudence was likely to be fortified by parental prohibition.

In the agricultural class in Japan, dowry was not normally a significant form of property.[g] The bride rarely took with her more than items of personal use, such as clothing, cosmetics, or a chest of drawers; and even if she took a sum of money (*jisankin*) or rights to land, these were usually trifling compared to what the groom stood to inherit in the form of house, furniture, heirlooms, land rights, and tools. Grooms thus had no reason to marry older women. Families with daughters had no means of enforcing a late marriage for them, and often no reason to. Some families nevertheless delayed a daughter's marriage in order to benefit from her earnings as a servant or from her labor and presence at home. But in doing so they

---

[g] In general, our information on the size and types of dowry in Tokugawa Japan is imprecise. But the examples cited by John Wigmore (*Law and Justice*, VII, 72–90) tend to bear out his general introductory statement that brides usually took only a chest of personal possessions with them, and that "but one bride out of a hundred" might bring money or land to her husband. A dowry of money or land seems to have been limited to wealthy families, to marriages of commoner women into *samurai* families, and to cases where the bride was especially ill-favored.

almost certainly lessened the girl's chances of marrying well; for as we have seen, the higher the economic status of families, the younger were the women their men took as brides.

Whether or not dowry—in effect, the allotment to women in the inheritance system—explains the different ages of female marriage in Nakahara and Europe, that disparity must have made marriage itself very different in the two societies. In Europe, women typically married at an age at which parents could not easily force an unwelcome partner on them; they came to their husbands with the benefit of greater maturity, more occupational experience, and often some years' experience working away from home. Owing to their youth, Nakahara brides were usually less able to assert themselves in the choice of a mate; they came to marriage less mature, less experienced occupationally, and virtually without property. Accordingly, the Nakahara woman's position in marriage was surely much weaker than the European. Or rather, it was so initially and for a certain time after marriage; then it began to improve, and may in the end have been more favorable in some ways than the European woman's position.

In fact, extreme youth compared to her husband, one of the conditions that made the Nakahara woman's position initially weak, served in time to turn the tables. As she and her husband grew older, as the husband's parents died and left only the couple and their children, the wife's youth by degrees became an advantage. At some point she became the more vigorous, competent, and confident of the pair—the person to whom others in the family might look for leadership and advice. One indication of this is that in a high proportion of Nakahara marriages the husband died first, and so was probably the first to feel infirmity. Indeed, the woman outlived her husband by eight years on average.[h]

One can translate this abstraction into concrete cases by following the histories of individual families in the village registers. Widowers with a married son, daughter-in-law, and grandchildren were rare; widows in that position were common. The registers tell

[h] The difference in life expectancy for females at age 20 and males at age 27.

us nothing explicitly about the lives of these female survivors. But a surprising number lived into their seventies or eighties, and a very few into their nineties. They occupied a position of honor in the register, appearing just after the family head; and at some point they might take on a Buddhist name in anticipation of death. They were already half spirit, a visible link between the living and the ancestors. One somehow senses that long before this they would have become a focus of family affection and pride in a way the husband rarely did.

Incomplete Marriages

Mean age at first marriage and the frequency of celibacy are not the only dimensions of nuptiality that affect fertility. We must also consider the frequency of marriages broken by death or divorce, whether either party (especially the woman) remarries, and if so, after how long an interval. Of 135 Nakahara marriages observed to termination, 53 percent were complete; that is, they lasted through the wife's fecund years (taken as ending at age 46). The remainder were *incomplete* by this definition. The causes of incomplete marriages are shown in Table 6.7. Death was the most common, not surprisingly, and was followed at a considerable distance by divorce.

As in other matters concerning marriage, we find significant class differences in the duration of marriage and the causes of termination. Middle- and upper-class marriages were almost twice as likely to be complete as lower-class, and when incomplete they were less likely to be broken by death. Four (possibly five) in ten lower-class marriages were incomplete owing to the death of one spouse, as compared to one in three marriages in the other classes. This was because of more favorable mortality in the middle and upper classes.[i] There was no significant difference in the incidence of divorce.

Class differences appear clearly in the ratio of widowers to

[i]Standardized crude death rates for married persons aged 20 to 60 in the three classes were 11.9 for the lower, 8.3 for the middle, and 7.7 for the upper class. These rates are standardized for ages on the entire population for 1717–1830.

TABLE 6.7

Causes of Termination in Incomplete First Marriages

First marriages*	Class			All (N = 135)
	Lower (N = 31)	Middle (N = 54)	Upper (N = 50)	
Complete	35%	57%	60%	53%
Incomplete, terminated by:				
Death of wife	19	9	2	9
Death of husband	23	17	28	22
Death of both spouses†	0	2	0	1
Divorce	6	9	6	7
Disappearance of wife	0	4	2	2
Disappearance of husband	6	0	0	1
Unknown cause	10	2	2	4

* Excludes eight marriages in the lower class, seven in the middle class, and four in the upper class that we cannot identify as complete or incomplete owing to termination of the record.
† Impossible to ascertain who had died first.

widows in incomplete marriages: this was about 1 to 1 in the lower class, 1 to 2 in the middle, and 1 to 14 in the upper. Table 6.8 suggests why. At equal ages of marriage for the husband, except ages 15–19, the age difference between spouses increased with the economic status of the husband. Husbands in the upper class, being older relative to their wives than those in the lower class, were that much more likely to die before them.

We had expected a higher rate of remarriage in incomplete marriages than we found. Only one in three widowers and one in five widows remarried. For both sexes, remarriage seems to have depended largely on whether there were children (Table 6.9). Both of the two childless widowers remarried, but only two of ten widowers with children. Two of four childless widows remarried; one returned to her native village and may have remarried; and only one clearly remained unmarried. However, only four of 25 widows with children remarried, and the conditions of remarriage are instructive. Three of the four remarried but remained in the husband's family: two married brothers-in-law, and one married an adopted husband brought into the family, presumably because the father-in-law, though alive, was too old (67) and the woman's son too young (5) to act as family head. The one widow with a child who married out of her husband's family did so only *after* the child's death.

Clearly, the operative cultural rule in Nakahara was that child-less widows could remarry; but widows with children could not, except in the husband's family, and the circumstances permitting this were unusual. Some possible reasons for the significance of children in this regard come to mind. Widows with children tended to be older than those without, and found it more difficult to re-marry for this reason. Perhaps more important, childless widows were not fully members of the husband's family; thus they were free to leave and possibly even encouraged to do so. Conversely, a widow could not take her children away from the husband's family,

TABLE 6.8
*Mean Difference in Age of Spouses in First Marriages,
by Husband's Age at Marriage and Economic Class*

Husband's age at marriage	Lower class		Middle class		Upper class	
	N	Mean	N	Mean	N	Mean
15–19	1	3.0	2	2.0	6	2.0
20–24	8	3.8	19	5.4	17	5.7
25–29	9	5.9	22	7.1	20	10.4
30–34	11	9.5	12	11.8	7	14.4
35 or more	11	12.4	6	14.5	4	15.0

NOTE: Means are mean differences in years between husbands' ages and wives'.

TABLE 6.9
*The Remarriage of Widows With and Without Children,
by Economic Class*

Condition	Widows with children		Widows without children	
	All	Remarrying	All	Remarrying
Class of deceased husband's family:				
Lower	6	1	1	0
Middle	5	1	4	1
Upper	13	2	1	1
TOTALS	24	4	6	2
Mean age at widowhood	37.6	27.8	27.2	24.0

to which they belonged. Also, as a full family member she herself had a generally recognized responsibility to stay in the family and work for its survival; and as a mother she could best secure her children's future in this way.

Divorce

The importance of children to the wife's position in the family appears again in divorce figures. Not counting instances where a wife or husband disappeared, we found nine cases of divorce classified as such by the registrar (considering first marriages only). Eight of the nine ended childless marriages, which lasted an average of 3.3 years, scarcely long enough to test the bride's fertility.[1] It would be a mistake, however, to assume that childlessness was the only significant ground for divorce; and probably there were often important secondary grounds. For example, how long a husband's family was willing to wait for a child appears to have depended in important part on how they felt about the wife, if we are to go by other Tokugawa cases.[2] How she felt about them was also important, for contrary to the usual impression, women in rural Japan often took the initiative in divorce.[3]

Six of the nine divorced husbands remarried, most of them within five years, and two others might have remarried if they had not died shortly after the divorce. The remaining husband lived a considerable time after his divorce without remarrying, but gave way as family head to his younger brother who had married. Whether there was a connection between failure to remarry and surrender of the headship (and if so, whether failure to remarry led to the surrender or vice versa) is uncertain, but it looks as though there were some link between the two.

What happened to the nine women after divorce cannot be ascertained, since they returned to their home villages and passed out of the Nakahara registers. However, we have the counterpart of these

---

[1]The distribution of complete first marriages by interval between marriage and first birth was:

Interval in years	0	1	2	3	4	5	6	7	8	9	10+
No. of marriages	3	10	17	14	8	5	1	3	1	0	2

women in 17 divorcées who returned to Nakahara from first marriages elsewhere. Eleven remarried after an average of 2.0 years;
four remained unmarried; one disappeared from Nakahara; and
one was age 24 when the record ended, and so may have remarried.

Thus most divorced women (between 65 and 76 percent) remarried, and most widows did not. The most important reason for the
difference would seem to be that widows were tied to their husband's families through children, whereas divorcées were not. Also
divorcées on the average were much younger than widows when the
marriages ended.[k] Since divorce usually ended a childless marriage
and resulted in a quick remarriage, it probably did not lower general fertility significantly, and may even have raised it slightly by
replacing a barren with a fruitful marriage. On the other hand, incomplete marriage through the death of one of the spouses unquestionably lowered fertility, since it was frequent and rather rarely
followed by remarriage.

The Sex Ratio and Nuptiality

We have seen that the probability of reaching age 50 without
marrying was 4 percent for women and 12 percent for men. This
considerable difference raises no special question in Nakahara,
where people often left or came into the village when marrying. But
it would raise a question in a closed population with demographic
characteristics identical to Nakahara's in all other ways. In that
case we would wonder how a higher proportion of women than
men could marry. There are two possible lines of explanation:
women may have married only once, whereas some men married
more than once, and some never; or there may have been more men
of marriageable age than women.[1]

We are obliged to discard the first alternative, since the ratio of

[k] The mean age of the 11 returning divorcées who remarried was 22.6 years. The
figure for childless widows was 27.2, and that for widows with children 37.6.

[1] A third line of explanation may occur to some readers, namely, the differential
mortality of the two sexes before marriage caused by the different time spans before
mean age at first marriage. But this can be ruled out immediately, for it would help
only if females married later than males; since they married earlier, this factor only
complicates explanation.

second marriages to all marriages was about the same for both sexes in Nakahara. The second alternative—more men of marriageable age than women—could occur in a closed population either by more women dying young than men or by fewer females being allowed to live at birth. Life expectancy in Nakahara at all ages was better for females than males (see Table 4.2), so the skewing of the sex ratio would have to originate at birth. In fact, we know that the sex ratio at registered birth in Nakahara was 114. This cannot be considered abnormal in a small population, but in a large population, where normal would be 102, it would represent a substantial skewing.[m]

This hypothetical situation is of some interest because the sex ratio in the entire Japanese population was 115 in 1732. Or rather, this was the ratio in the registered population; it may have been not the actual ratio but a statistical artifact resulting from the underregistration of females. As will be seen later, there are strong reasons for discounting this possibility. If we do so, and if we also discount differential mortality as an explanation, we must consider the probable skewing of the sex ratio at birth through an overall bias against females in the practice of infanticide. This is not a wholly speculative possibility, since from literary and legal evidence this bias seems likely.

The reader will understand that this chain of reasoning is built on a series of assumptions, and only time will tell how realistic they are. Still, the exercise serves to bring out one possible effect of infanticide on fertility that is suggested by Nakahara when we think of its population, hypothetically, as large and closed. The immediate effect of infanticide on fertility is obviously to reduce the number of children born (or allowed to live). But if fewer females are allowed to live than males, there will also be a long-term indirect effect on fertility through nuptiality. That is, in each birth cohort, owing to the deficit of females, there will be a lower marriage rate than if the sex ratio was normal. The effect would be the same as if the sex

[m] We use 102 as normal rather than the more usual 105 to account for the change brought about by infant deaths before the average registration at standard age 1. See p. 60.

ratio were normal but a certain proportion of women never married or had children. The magnitude of this effect would depend on how skewed the sex ratio was at birth. If it was as high in a large closed population as in Nakahara, and as high as the sex ratio of the registered national population in 1732 suggests, this indirect effect could have been very strong indeed.

Conclusions

We may now summarize briefly our principal findings concerning nuptiality in Nakahara.

1. With rare exceptions, only males who were or became family heads married. This rule, which seems designed to prevent the fragmentation of holdings, raised the proportion of males never married by age 50 to over 10 percent. The further tendency to postpone male marriage until actual or imminent succession to the headship kept the mean age of first marriage for males relatively high. By contrast, early and nearly universal marriage was the rule for women.

2. Both men and women tended to marry younger in upper-class than in lower-class families. The differential was considerably greater for women than men, apparently because male marriage was closely linked to succession to the family headship, whereas female marriage was manipulable within broad limits for economic and other reasons of family advantage.

3. A substantial number of marriages were incomplete owing to the death of one spouse. For both widows and widowers, remarriage seems to have depended mainly on whether there were children: when there were, as was usual, remarriage was uncommon; when there were none, remarriage was likely. This was a significant check on fertility in Nakahara.

4. Marriages in the middle and upper classes had a much better chance of completion than those in the lower class, owing to the more favorable mortality in those classes. For this reason, as well as later female marriage in the lower class, fertility became substantially lower as one went down the economic scale. This accounts for the tendency, which we observe in the next chapter, for poor fam-

ilies to die out biologically. Often, they were replaced in the village by new families founded as branches by upper-class families, which probably contributed significantly to the social peace of the community. This is not to say that Nakahara was free of strife. But property tended in nearly all periods to concentrate in the hands of a limited number of families; and without the constant founding of new families with property and the constant erosion of propertyless families, strife would surely have been much sharper.

5. Nearly 10 percent of all marriages ended in divorce. Divorce was limited almost exclusively to childless marriages; it generally occurred at a young age for women; and in most cases both parties quickly remarried.

6. A powerful check on fertility may have been a deficit of females in the general population as the result of an overall bias against females in the practice of infanticide. This possibility, barely hinted at in Nakahara, is worth testing in a larger population. Such testing might add a new dimension to our understanding of the slow growth of Japanese population in the latter half of the To-kugawa period. It might also lead to new and interesting questions concerning the relations of sex ratio, nuptiality, and fertility. For if nuptiality and fertility were affected by an abnormally high sex ratio in the national population in 1732, we must ask how they were affected by the gradual convergence of the sex ratio toward normal between 1732 and 1872. This is a question to which we will briefly return in the final chapter.

Chapter Seven   Family and Farming

T HE PATTERNS of apparent infanticide in Nakahara suggest that it was practiced partly as an instrument of family planning: which is to say, infanticide followed rules that required both foresight to use and a conscious design of benefit to the families involved. This chapter attempts to explain the planning element in infanticide by exploring the relationship between the family where decisions about children were made and the farm where the family's living was made. We do not attempt to explain *why* infanticide was practiced—only the "rules" of its practice. In the same way, we might attempt to explain certain business behavior in terms of profits without raising the question of why profits are sometimes valued above other things. The question of why infanticide was practiced in Nakahara is an obviously important one; but to answer it would require a quite different kind of investigation and more knowledge than we have of Nakaharan views of life and death.

Family and Farming

To say that family and farming were interdependent in Nakahara does not sufficiently convey the closeness of the relationship. Farming, with its allied tasks, was the principal occupation and nearly the sole source of income for most families, and its rhythms defined the annual cycle of work, rest, and worship. Severe annual variations in the harvest reverberated through family life, determining whether the family ate well or meagerly, whether the old might live another winter, whether a daughter could marry at the New Year.

As we shall see, farming in Nakahara was intensely competitive, with land changing hands continually in response to even very small setbacks and successes. Few families worked exactly the same land for many years running. Fields were lost in bad years, added in good, and good and bad years sometimes came in clutches. In a decade or two holdings could double in size or melt away to nothing. Families who lost their land usually continued to farm as tenants, adding rent to the burden of taxes.[a] However, this was often the prelude to ruin and demise; for families with land tended to survive, and those without it tended sooner or later to go out of existence. Ultimately, the competition for land was a competition for family survival.

When a family could no longer survive as a group, its members dispersed, and its identity was lost. House and chattels were sold, name and reputation forgotten, graves in the village neglected and overgrown. Family corporate life lapsed with the lapse of the ancestral ceremonies that linked the living and the dead and projected both into the future; and what had endowed man's work and suffering with significance in an orderly scheme of things gave way to chaos. Thus the struggle for family survival was not just a struggle to stay alive, but a struggle to give meaning to life itself:

If a man is foolish and brings his family [ie] to ruin, he commits a crime against his parents that will last for generations. But if the lessons of hard work and good farming are not forgotten, a man's conduct will conform to Heaven's way, and he will achieve the greatest filial piety.[1]

Just as the rhythms and fortunes of farming influenced the family, so those of the family influenced farming. Labor came almost exclusively from family members, and labor was the most important factor of production in Tokugawa farming. Tools were simple, and animals of limited use; the only capital of importance was housing and improvements in land, both of which were embodiments of past family labor. Farming efficiency therefore depended overwhelmingly on the size, age, sex, skill, motivation, and disci-

---

[a] Tenants normally did not pay the land tax directly; rather, it was included in the rent they paid the landholder. By "family" we mean here and elsewhere the basic landholding group and village-residential unit. Even without land the kinship group itself might persist, perhaps elsewhere and with a new basis for unity.

pline of all the members of the family. In the words of a "certain peasant" speaking to an eighteenth-century writer in southwestern Japan:

If one has 15 *tan* of paddy and can work it with family labor, the yield will be 25 bales of rice and 30 bales of winter wheat. With this the family can continue. But if he increases his land by 5 *tan*, he will no longer be able to cultivate entirely with family labor. He will have to hire a servant, acquire an ox, and buy fertilizer. Now his yield will be about 30 bales of rice and 40 of wheat, an overall increase of 15 bales. But when he subtracts the additional costs, his net return will be much less than formerly. Indeed, the year he increases his holding and hires labor he will suffer a deficit, and that year he must begin to borrow money.[2]

A contemporary writer on agriculture advised families on how to make their children into good farmers:

From the age of 8 boys should gather grass for the animals, pick up horse dung from the road, make rope, and help with other light work. When they work well, they should be praised and given a coin. When coins accumulate to a sufficient sum, the children should be allowed to buy something they want. Also, when they are given clothes they should be told it is a reward for work. Thus their childish hearts will develop the spirit of industry and perseverance. If they are given suitable work in this way when young and taught farming skills as they get older, by age 14 or 15 they will be industrious and meticulous farmers.[3]

Family size and membership were as important to farming success as skill and hard work. Too small a family could not meet the peaks of labor demand; one too large meant excessive costs, perhaps hunger. A family should contain at least one married couple, to ensure the proper sexual division of labor as well as biological continuity. And there should be more than one generation of adults, to combine the advantages of youthful vigor and mature experience. These conditions were difficult to fulfill optimally over a long period of time, since families were constantly changing through accident, illness, maturation, aging, death, departure, marriage, and birth. All these events altered farming capabilities, which were never exactly the same from one year to the next.

Capabilities changed greatly as the family changed. As families passed through the succession of generations, they also passed through a cycle of farming efficiency. In one full generation efficiency typically went from low to high and then back to low. This had a powerful influence on the distribution of land in a village, since families did not pass through their cycles in phase. One would be at peak efficiency while another was at the nadir; one would approach the peak as another descended from it; and whatever the relative situation at a given moment, it was bound to change. Unlike modern businesses, among whom comparative advantages are often long-term, farm families in Nakahara were not likely to enjoy an advantage over their neighbors for many years running. The only exceptions were the few families whose political and financial power became so great that it did not much matter whether they farmed well or badly.

The impact of family on farming can be seen in documents that transfer or mortgage houses and land. These transactions were seldom voluntary on the part of the owner but were almost always a response to emergencies. The owner, who was the principal signator and from whose point of view the instrument was written, often alluded in the document to the reasons for his present plight, as though apologizing. The reasons were almost invariably family trouble: [4]

Although we have lived in this house for many years, our situation has been difficult; and when my husband died this summer, our situation became still worse.

We bought this house and land some years ago, but now my son Sensuke has died.

Because of illness I have had difficulty paying taxes in recent years, and now. . . .

Because my wife has left me. . . .

Although families were thus always changing in ways that affected their farming, they could exert a limited control over the cycle—and thus improve farming efficiency—by the deliberate inclusion, exclusion, or retention of family members. The means of *inclusion* (or family expansion) were marriage, procreation, adoption in, hiring of servants, or amalgamation with another family.

The means of *exclusion* (reduction) were divorce, abortion, infanticide, adoption out, sending members out to work, dismissal of servants, or splitting off a branch family. Families could also retain late or release early members who would in any case leave sooner or later to marry or find a job. Decisions on these matters were being made constantly, if only in deciding to do nothing for the time being. Thus conscious decisions affected farming no less than the involuntary changes brought about by death, accident, and aging; and it is our belief that these decisions were very often made in the interest of farm efficiency.

Restrictions on the Movement of Land

The competition for land exerted a constant pressure on family decision-making. We tend to think of such competition as a result of the commercialization of farming, and certainly commercialization does promote competition. However, there was intense competition in Nakahara, where there is no sign of significant commercialization; and we believe this was probably true of many Tokugawa villages. Competition was in part the result of family farming (which meant not only different but constantly varying capabilities among farm units) combined with two characteristic conditions of Japanese agriculture in the eighteenth century.

One of these was the essentially fixed amount of available land. Arable land could be expanded in two ways only: by the more intensive use of existing fields (reducing fallow time), or by bringing new land under cultivation. Neither was possible on any large scale. Fields were everywhere cropped annually; in regions where weather permitted, many fields were double- or even triple-cropped. The major sources of fertilizer—fish, night soil, and grass or leaves from untilled land—were already being fully exploited, and multiple cropping could not be significantly increased without new sources. Nor was it possible with the existing technology to bring new land under cultivation: the remaining land was generally marginal and costly to use, and every extension of cultivated area decreased the supply of fertilizer, endangering the maintenance of annual cropping on existing fields.

In most parts of the country, then, it was impossible for a family to acquire additional land except from another farm family by purchase, loan, or foreclosure. This condition in itself did not mean necessarily that land would move from hand to hand in direct response to changes in farming efficiency, for transfer may have been impeded by various technical or institutional obstacles. For example, the size of the smallest available units of land, which has varied greatly from one preindustrial society to another, may have been too large for easy transfer. Or the majority of peasant families may have been subject to legal restrictions making it difficult or impossible for them to acquire land, however excellent their farming.

These illustrations bring us to the second feature of Tokugawa agriculture: the weakness of restraints on the transfer of land. Some comparisons at this point may be helpful.

An important impediment to land transfer in many preindustrial societies is the claim of kinship, which tends to limit the consequence of inequalities between individuals and families. We would expect to observe this effect especially in the relations of main and branch families, which in Nakahara usually resulted from the partitioning of a property between a father and a son, or between an older and a younger brother. The division of property was almost always extremely unequal: main family shares in Nakahara averaged 23.1 *koku* of arable land, and branch family shares only 10.4.[b] Property other than land was divided even more unequally; and the house, farmyard, and heirlooms usually went intact to the main family. Since the median holding for the whole period of observation in Nakahara was 12 *koku*, it is clear that main and branch families typically belonged to different economic strata, from which circumstance we might expect that in time of trouble substantial help would flow from main to branch families, cush-

[b] As explained in Chapter 2, MC, or tax registers giving the size of holdings in *koku*, were available for ten scattered dates. Comparing the figures for main and branch family holdings in the first MC after fission yields the average holding figures given. Of the 55 cases of division into main and branch families between 1717 and 1830, ten occurred after our last list of holding size (1823), and in six other cases information on holding size is deficient. Thus the averages given represent 39 cases of family branching.

ioning the effects of competition. But observation does not confirm this. Main-family holdings often grew after the partitioning, whereas branch-family holdings shrank; and branch families passed out of existence at a rate of 7.4 per thousand family-years, as compared to 2.65 for main families.[5] Altogether, the impression is that mutual aid among kin in Nakahara was limited and that each family's fate was essentially in its own hands.[c]

There was nothing in Tokugawa Japan closely comparable to the kind of restraint imposed on competition in medieval Europe by the open-field system of agriculture, with its communal regulation of crops, planting, harvesting, and fallowing. Tokugawa farmers were not wholly free of communal controls: they could irrigate only at certain times, in prescribed amounts, and in a fixed rotation. These controls, vigorously enforced, did restrict the intensity of land use and the choice of crops. But plant varieties, which were constantly being experimented with, were a matter of choice; and methods of tillage, harvest dates, winter crops, and unirrigated land were all free of regulation. Authorities above the village level often forbade, or demanded, the planting of certain crops, especially on paddy; but these efforts depended on the village headmen for enforcement and were largely ineffective. All in all, there was little to prevent one family's farming better than another—often very much better—and such differences were soon felt in the distribution of land.

Again by contrast with Europe, no large amount of land in Tokugawa Japan was locked away in aristocratic estates whose owners were protected in their possession by legal privileges, tax immunities, or political influence. By the eighteenth century nearly all farm land was effectively owned by commoners, all but a few of whom were legally peasants (*nō*). *Samurai* title to land was limited to the right to collect taxes, or rather, to receive a share of the taxes levied and collected by the *daimyō*'s officials. Although lords were concerned to prevent the concentration of landholding among the peasants and attempted to restrict its transfer, they never discovered

[c] Of the 17 branch families that died out, seven disappeared within 20 years of their establishment, when the relationship between main and branch families should still have been affectively close.

a way of making their restrictions effective, and had largely abandoned them in practice by the nineteenth century. As a result, village landlords were common. But most held very small amounts of land (a holding of over 100 acres was extremely rare); they paid taxes like other holders, and could maintain possession only through efficient exploitation.

Rarely was the transfer of land within the village impeded by the size, location, or shape of fields. Fields were small and almost infinitely divisible or combinable. Animals were not much used in farming, and Professor Hayami has shown that their role on the Nobi plain was declining with time; thus fields did not necessarily have to be of a size or shape to accommodate a single horse and plow, let alone a team. Farmland did not have to be combined with pasture, as good farming practice required in parts of Europe; nor was it necessary for plots of the same holding to lie together. Holdings were widely dispersed in any case, as the result of partitioning between heirs, and any piece of land that might be acquired was likely to be near one already worked by the family; if not, it could be tenanted to a family for whom the location was more convenient. In short, for any given plot the members of the entire village were, spatially, potential holders.

The Spirit of Competition in Farming

Historians and anthropologists have emphasized the solidarity of the traditional Japanese farming village, and unquestionably solidarity was one of its major characteristics. Exchange of labor between neighbors and kin was the rule; compromise and accommodation were highly valued; universal observance of holidays and festivals was enforced. Speech, clothing, farm tools, custom, and religious observances all differed between villages but were remarkably homogeneous within them. Dissent from village opinion on important issues brought ostracism or expulsion. Even today hamlets (*buraku*), which are descended from Tokugawa villages, tend to vote as groups.

But there was an equally important competitive side to village life that has been largely ignored: a competition between families rather than individuals, covert rather than open, but fierce and unrelenting nevertheless. Farming was the arena of conflict, and the tools of victory were skill, ingenuity, hard work, and perseverance. The immediate goal was the improvement of family well-being and village status—the last explicitly recognized in seating arrangements, offices, rank-titles, and privileges with respect to dress and domestic architecture. These signs of status, which were often formal and even constitutional, were not automatically readjusted as economic status changed, and bitter quarrels sometimes erupted over the resulting discrepancies.[6]

Tokugawa writers on agriculture remark on the competitiveness of farming in many passages. It may be objected that they were describing how farmers *ought* to behave to get ahead, not necessarily depicting reality; but this literary advice was remarkably consistent with peasant behavior in the land market. The writers were not themselves peasants, of course; most were rich farmers, often educated and well-traveled. But they lived and traveled among the peasants, stopping at farmhouses to inquire about crops, plant varieties, and yields, collecting seeds, and comparing methods in one place with those in another. And they declared their intention of writing for the peasants (many of whom were literate), adopting a simple style of writing suitable to the purpose and illustrating their texts with beguiling sketches of rural scenes as well as how-to-do-it drawings. Above all, they talked (with only occasional lapses) about things peasants were concerned with—seeds, fertilizers, tools, and especially how to make one's family wealthy.

One of the earliest Tokugawa works on agriculture spoke of the difference skill and effort made to a family: "[If a man takes soil, seeds, and planting dates carefully into account, fertilizes properly, and does all other work conscientiously,] he can get 1.4 or 1.5 *koku* of rice per *tan* on land normally yielding 1.0 *koku*; whereas a negligent neighbor on the same land will get only 0.7 or 0.8 *koku*."[7]

Concerning the larger consequences of these differences, a village headman wrote: "In farming, those who are skillful and work hard profit, those who are clumsy or lazy lose, and from this circumstance arise the differences between families of wealth and poverty." And he added, so that no one would miss the point: "Wealth brings happiness and poverty sadness."[8] A jingle appearing in a book on sericulture offered much the same message: "When others clean the silkworm trays once, you do it twice. When they feed the worms thrice, you feed them four times."[9]

A famous book on farm tools and equipment, which discusses the relative advantages and disadvantages of each item, summarizes the recommendation of a farmer concerning *tsuranuki*, a footgear made of leather that the man said he wore instead of straw sandals:

Besides this, *tsuranuki* have other advantages over straw sandals. Since they are warmer, one can go into the fields earlier in the morning and can work better because the feet are supple. This is no great advantage for a single day, but over a year and a lifetime it makes a big difference. It also saves the cost of hot water for washing the feet daily.[10]

A village headman described the value of keeping a detailed written record (which, judging from surviving copies, many farmers in fact did) of crops, planting dates, yields, and so on:

Let the farmer keep such a record for cotton, tobacco, and all other crops. He will then have a record for each crop of good years and bad. By consulting it he will recall the past; his losses will again sear his soul, and his successes warm the cockles of his heart. From this experience [presumably fortifying his will] he will necessarily become a better farmer.[11]

Morality tales often had a place in books on farming:

A certain person in Usui District in Jōshū lost his father when young and served his mother faithfully. The family was poor and did not even light a fire in the morning and evening. So mother and child passed their days in want. Having exhausted all means of caring for his mother, the young man determined that nothing brought a greater profit to farmers than sericulture. He therefore studied the secrets of raising worms, and, hoping to provide a comfortable life for his mother and wife and children, he planted mulberry bushes on a part of his land. He then listened carefully to successful sericulturists in his village and nearby as they discussed the pros and cons of the various methods of raising silkworms. He began raising worms himself, working at the task night and day, and in five or six years his profits increased. He bought up arable fields and forest land and became one of the wealthiest men in the vicinity of Takasaki. This was the "virtue" [*toku*, a word that also means "profit"] of filial piety.[12]

It is not surprising that the family assumes so prominent a place in stories like this. In fact, contemporary writers often stressed the importance of family and the upbringing of children to a farming household:

Nothing is more important than raising children. From the age of five or six, children in poor families should be made to look after the younger children, help with spinning, and work in the fields. As adults they will then not be afraid of work, and through diligence may come to own land.[13]

Since this is an era of increasing prices, if a man does not get the maximum yield from his crops, he will be unable to perpetuate his family [ie] and to support his wife and children. Let him pray to the gods that his children will surpass others [hito ni kosu] and thereby get on in life. For if they do not—if they let his hopes come to nothing and by indolence ruin the family —how great will his crime then be.[14]

The Mobility of Land

Land circulated continuously among competing peasant families, not only in Nakahara but in much of the country. Tanaka Kyūgu, a district official and the son of a village headman, wrote of his native Kantō in the early eighteenth century that village tax registers typically became illegible owing to emendations after approximately ten years, so often did plots change hands. He added that many old and distinguished Kantō families had lost their property and died out, and that new families, some founded by men who had first come into the village as servants, had taken their place at the top of village hierarchies.

If this seems an exaggeration, look at the change in the size of holdings from one tax register to the next in Nakahara, an average interval of twelve years:[d]

	N	Percent
No change	65	17%
Increased or decreased by 10 percent or less	78	21
Increased or decreased by 11–20 percent	46	12
Increased or decreased by more than 20 percent	188	50

[d] Each holding in the 377 cases listed here represents a holding during one interval of observation. Thus a holding in existence throughout the period and listed in all

Even these figures understate the amount of change, since 42 of the 65 cases of no change were nil holders—families without land—at both observations. Eliminating these cases reduces the proportion of holdings remaining unchanged between observations to 7 percent.

Not all changes in holding size reflected the transfer of land from one Nakahara family to another, of course. Some changes may represent land brought under cultivation for the first time, or taken out of cultivation as a result of damage from flooding; and holdings also changed size through partitioning between main and branch families. But most changes—probably 60 percent—were the result of the transfer of land between village families (see Appendix C).

We have already seen (Chapter 3) that landholding in Naka-hara concentrated markedly over the whole period, but especially after 1780. Although large holdings were thereby growing at the expense of small and medium, we must not imagine a discrete group of large holdings that were growing continuously. There were frequent changes in the membership of the top group, with new families entering from below and old families dropping out. Only two or three families were large holders at all observations, and there was proportionately as much turnover in the ranks of small and medium holders.

Table 7.1 summarizes the degree of change and continuity in holding size among various classes of holders. For each of four classes—large, medium, small, and landless—it shows the proportion of families in the class at one observation who were still in it at the next one, and also the proportion who had moved into each of the other classes. For example, by looking down the first column on the left, we see that there was a total of 146 large holdings at all observations together, and that 76 percent of this number were still

---

ten MC registers would be considered as nine holdings, one for each separate observed interval. We exclude five cases where a family, although in existence, was not listed as holding land at either the first or second of successive observations; we also exclude cases where a family went out of existence between the first observation and the second.

TABLE 7.1
*Changes of Individual Holdings in Class from
One Landholding Observation to Next*

Class of holding at next observation	Class of holding at first observation			
	Large	Medium	Small	Landless
Large	76% (111)	14% (19)	5% (3)	0% (0)
Medium	19% (28)	61% (86)	10% (6)	3% (2)
Small	1% (2)	12% (17)	45% (26)	6% (4)
Landless	3% (4)	8% (11)	26% (15)	63% (45)
Demised family	1% (1)	5% (7)	14% (8)	28% (20)
All holdings	100% (146)	100% (140)	100% (58)	100% (71)

NOTE: Figures in parentheses indicate number of cases.

large at the next observation; 19 percent were medium, 1 percent small, 3 percent landless, and 1 percent had gone out of existence (demised). This illustrates the extraordinary difficulty that large holders had in keeping their place in the village. Small holders had even more difficulty: 40 percent of them at one observation either were landless or had demised at the next one. Nevertheless, the highest probability was still to remain in the same class; note that the highest values are on the diagonal of the matrix.

Clearly, for holders of any class it was easier to move down the scale than up. But it was possible to move up. Fourteen percent of medium holders, 15 percent of small, and 9 percent of landless families moved to a higher class between observations. Also, as becomes clear when we follow individual holdings over several observations, few holdings grew or declined steadily over long periods. Most underwent both ups and downs, even when their long-term trend was strongly one way. Figure 7.1 illustrates this tendency in a selection of holdings of different size.

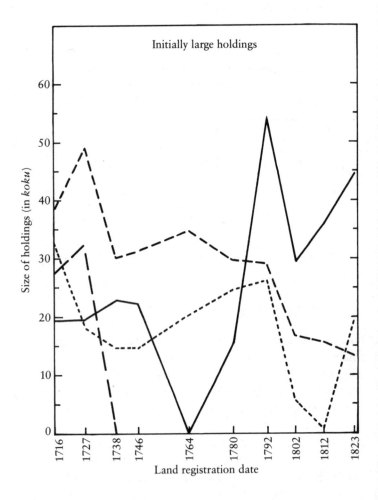

Fig. 7.1. Change over time in size of selected holdings. *Above*: initially large holdings. *Opposite, top*: initially medium holdings. *Opposite, bottom*: initially small holdings.

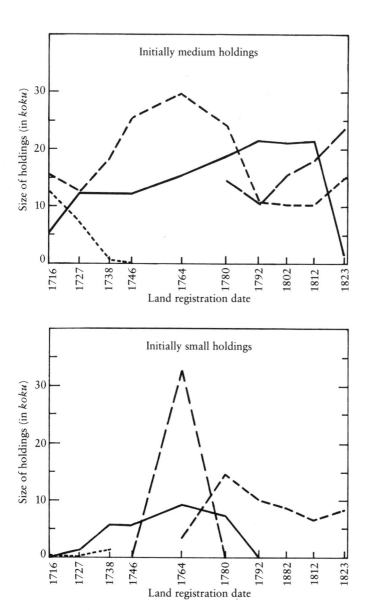

Holding Size and Family Size

If the competition for land was in part a competition of families to adjust their size and composition to the requirements of farming, one would expect to find a positive correlation between family size and holding size. Of course, such a correlation could come about without intention on the part of families, through the effects of differential fecundity or mortality—though this seems unlikely in view of the continual change in the size of holdings. Fecundity and mortality could hardly be so variable, and the presumption would therefore be that there was some conscious adjustment of family size. Failure to find a positive correlation, however, would not necessarily disprove the idea of deliberate family adjustment. As we have repeatedly stressed, holdings were ownership, not farming, units, and the exigencies of farming, we believe, were the major influence on family size. Holdings and farms diverged through the letting and renting of land, and the divergence probably increased over time with the concentration of landholding. If we find no correlation, therefore, it may simply be because holdings mirrored actual farming badly; but if we find one, it would be despite this fact.

The correlations between landholding and family size at the ten observation dates for landholding were:[e]

Date	Corre-lation	Date	Corre-lation
1717	0.71	1780	0.57
1727	0.49	1792	0.38
1738	0.49	1802	0.44
1746	0.50	1812	0.19
1764	0.69	1823	0.13

As one would expect with so much change in landholding, the correlation varies considerably by date; but it is highly significant (at a level of 0.005) at all dates except the last two.

[e] Family size, here and elsewhere, includes all persons registered as living in the family during the year specified. This will include servants as well as family members; however, family members registered as working as servants elsewhere (and thus not living with the family that year) are not included in calculations of mean family size.

What was happening through time can be seen in Table 7.2 and Figure 7.2, which show mean family size for small, medium, and large holders at each of the ten observation dates for landholding. Although mean family size varied significantly with holding size and tended to increase at all levels of landholding, class differences in family size narrowed conspicuously after 1780 and disappeared in 1812 and 1823.

Does this mean that the labor requirements of farming ceased to exert a significant influence on family size at the end of the observation period? We think not, since such a development would have required an increase in employment outside farming, and there is no sign of that. Indeed, such employment seems to have been contracting, since the number of servants inside Nakahara and the number of Nakaharans employed as servants elsewhere both declined in the late eighteenth century, and both groups of servants almost completely disappeared from the record after 1800.

It is more likely that the tax registers became less and less reliable as a guide to how land was actually farmed. We know that

TABLE 7.2

Mean Family Size of Small, Medium, and Large Holders, 1716–1823

Year	Holding							
	Small	Medium		Large		All	
	family size	family size	(Index)*	family size	(Index)	family size	(Index)
1716	1.6	2.5	(156)	4.1	(256)	3.0	(188)
1727	2.5	2.9	(116)	3.8	(152)	3.2	(128)
1738	2.7	3.8	(141)	5.1	(189)	3.8	(141)
1746	2.5	4.5	(180)	5.9	(236)	4.5	(180)
1764	2.8	4.5	(161)	6.2	(221)	4.9	(175)
1780	3.0	4.3	(143)	5.6	(187)	4.6	(153)
1792	3.8	4.8	(126)	5.4	(142)	4.6	(121)
1802	4.0	4.5	(113)	5.8	(145)	4.7	(118)
1812	5.1	5.0	(98)	5.7	(112)	5.2	(102)
1823	4.9	5.1	(104)	5.4	(110)	5.1	(104)
1716–1823	3.7	4.2	(114)	5.3	(143)	4.4	(119)

NOTE: Small holders have 0–4 *koku*; medium holders, 4.1–18.0 *koku*; large holders over 18.0 *koku*. These rather arbitrary definitions of class give groups of nearly equal membership for all ten dates combined (bottom row).
* Figures in parentheses are index numbers based on 100 for small holders.

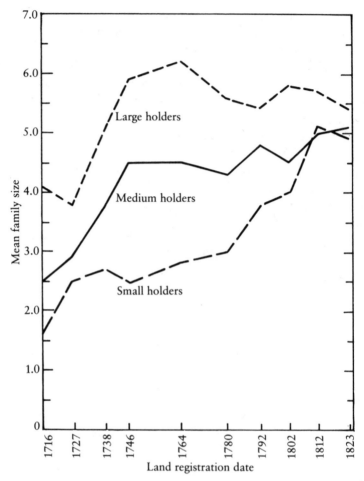

Fig. 7.2. Mean family size by holding size

after 1780 there was a dramatic increase in the concentration of land in the hands of large holders at the expense of medium and small. This was caused almost entirely by the expansion of the holding of family number 14, the village headman's family, which descended from the founder of the village. As a result, the number of small holders and landless families in the village increased from 8 to 27—or from 17 percent to 51 percent of all families.

Holding	1780		1823	
	N	Percent	N	Percent
Large	17	36%	10	19%
Medium	22	46	15	30
Small	8	17	27	51
TOTAL	47	99	52	100

The families who lost their land to family number 14 probably continued to work the same land as before, though now in whole or in part as the headman's tenants. This would have drastically reduced their size as holders, but would have left their size as farmers—and presumably as families—unchanged, thus upsetting the earlier relationship in the village between family size and holding size. In short, in 1812 and 1823, we see not a breakdown in the relations of family and farming but a radical divergence between land holding (registration) and land use.

Family Entries and Exits and Changes in Holding Size

Theoretically, one way of testing the hypothesis of deliberate family adjustment is to observe the flow of exits and entries in relation to changes in holding size. In practice, this is difficult for two reasons. One is that we can observe holdings only at registered intervals of eight to eighteen years, and therefore can observe the timing of changes in holding size only very roughly. The other is that holding size, as just noted, often changed without a corresponding change in farm size, particularly after 1780.

Nevertheless, we arranged the data to see if there was any relationship between family exits and entries on the one hand and changes in holding size on the other. First, we calculated the percentage change in size for each holding during each interval of observation. Then, pooling all observations of change, we classified holdings into growing, stable, and declining groups, which were defined respectively as growing by 10 percent or more, neither growing nor declining by as much as 10 percent, and declining by 10 percent or more.[15] Finally, for each of these groups we computed the rate of family entries and exits per 1,000 family-years during the relevant intervals. Table 7.3 summarizes the results.

TABLE 7.3
Entries and Exits from Families with Increasing,
Decreasing, and Stable Holdings

| | Holding size | | |
Category	Increasing	Stable	Decreasing
Family-years	539	643	928
Exits per 1,000 family-years			
All exits	168.8	219.3	243.5
All except death	63.1	119.8	144.4
Deaths	105.7	99.5	99.1
Entries per 1,000 family-years	205.9	233.3	237.1
Entry rate minus exit rate	37.1	14.0	− 6.4

NOTE: Observation periods average 11.7 years.

Families with growing holdings had a lower exit rate than those with stable holdings, and those with stable holdings a lower rate than those with declining holdings. If we exclude deaths in order to limit observation to voluntary exits, the difference between rates increases to a significance level of 0.001.[16] This is what one would expect if families had adjusted their size to changes in holding size. Families with growing holdings would tend to hold members, and those with declining holdings would tend to lose them. But the results ran contrary to expectation when it came to entries; families with growing holdings turned out to have fewer entries than families with stable or declining holdings. However, the differences are not significant, and the net rate of family change (entry rate minus exit rate) runs in the right direction, with families on growing holdings growing more than two-and-a-half times as fast as families with stable holdings, and with families on declining holdings growing negatively.

These data do not necessarily mean that families were always adjusted in size as holding size changed; instead, holding size may have been altered through the sale or purchase of land in response to changes in family size. The direction of the causation cannot be clear from the statistics alone. Probably influence did run both ways, but in any case it ran powerfully from holding to family. We have just noted that voluntary exits—excluding deaths—were the critical factor in differential change in families with growing, stable, and declining holdings. The question therefore is whether families with declining holdings typically sold land in response to uncontrolled exits, or controlled exits to match the untoward loss of land. The second was in all likelihood the more common mode of adjustment. It was a simple matter in many families to reduce size by dismissing a servant, sending a son out to work, or hastening a daughter's marriage. But in view of the intense competition for land, it is hard to see why families not forced to do so financially would sell land merely because they were temporarily short of labor, since it was possible to let land to tenants in plots of almost any size. (It should be remembered that letting land to tenants would not change the holding sizes in our data.)

Holding Size and Family Demise

Behind the apparently continuous adjustment of family size and composition to the needs of farming was the stark fact that only the more successful farm families survived. Families were continually going out of existence and new families being founded (see Chapter 3, Figure 3.2). Of a total of 100 Nakahara families under observation in 1717 or after, more than one-third were not in existence in 1830.[f] Few, if any, of the demising families moved away voluntarily; most eroded away through deaths and abandonments, and nearly all were landless by the time of their demise. The sizes of holdings among demising families for whom we have a landholding observation prior to demise were:[17]

Holding in *koku*	Number of families
Less than 2.0	25
2.0 to 5.0	5
5.1 to 13.0	4
13.1 to 15.0	2
Over 15	1

[f] Of the 40 families in the 1717 register, 21 had gone out of existence by 1830. Nineteen of the 56 branch families set up during this period failed to survive through 1830, and two of the four families that moved in from other villages after 1717 also disappeared by 1830. Thus a total of 42 of the 100 families in our record had demised by 1830.

TABLE 7.4
Rate of Family Demise by Initial Landholding Size

First recorded holding size (*koku*)	Number of families	Demises	Demises per 1,000 family years
0–2	24	16	17.60
2–5	8	5	16.03
5–12	10	6	10.95
12–15	11	4	6.63
15–18	9	3	4.26
18–24	9	2	2.41
24–30	7	1	1.64
over 30	7	0	0

NOTE: The initial holding size is that of 1716 for families already in existence in 1717, and the first landholding listing after founding for all later families. There are no observations on holding size at all for 14 families (for example, those founded after 1823, our last listing); and one family is not included in the table because it is missing from the first listing following its founding.

Among the landless demisers were many families that at one time had held considerable land, but rarely did a family demise with a currently substantial holding.

Land was clearly critical to survival. Despite the movement of families up and down the holding scale, the size of a holding (including no holding) at any given time was an excellent predictor of the family's survival chances. This comes out clearly if we classify families by holding size at their first appearance in the land register, then calculate the demise rate (per 1,000 family-years) for various classes of holders (see Table 7.4 and Figure 7.3). The chances of demise, it will be seen, varied inversely with the size of the holding: the smaller the holding, the greater the danger of demise. This was true at every level of size. The family with even a slightly larger holding always had the better chance of survival.

Although the demise rate mounts as we go down the holding scale, the relation between size and demise was not a simple one. Many small holders or landless families survived over long periods, and a few made their way a respectable distance up the holding scale; on the other hand, some large holders lost land over a period of years and finally disappeared. The immediately operative factor in failure may often have been the loss of coherence and balance as a family. Consider Table 7.5, which summarizes certain features of demising families at various points in time prior to their demise.

Ten years before demise, these families were already undersized even for small holders, averaging 2.7 members as compared to 3.7 members for all small holders during the period 1717–1830. Given their other characteristics, a large proportion cannot have been effective farming units, and the proportion in this state increased with time. One year before demise, average family size was 1.5, 71 percent were single-member families, and over half had no male of working age.

How did families come to this pass? One of the obvious ways was by failing to recruit or hold brides. Seven of the families (all founded as branches) at no time in their history succeeded in bringing in a bride; another five lost the last bride through divorce soon after marriage; one saw the last marriage broken by the husband's

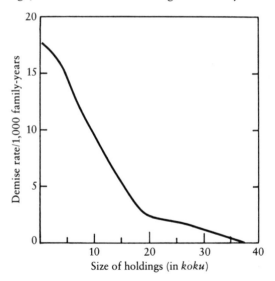

Fig. 7.3. Risks of family demise by amount of land held. The graph was plotted by using the mean holding size in each group of holdings rather than the midpoint.

TABLE 7.5
*Characteristics of Demising Families at Various Intervals
Prior to Demise*

| | Years before demise | | |
Family characteristic	10 years (N = 34)	5 years (N = 41)	1 year (N = 42)
Mean size	2.74	2.12	1.55
Single-member families	20%	39%	71%
No male aged 20–55	32	44	52
No female aged 20–55	35	44	62
No married couple	48	68	85

NOTE: All 42 demising families are included. Short-lived families account for the smaller number of families at ten and five years as compared to one year before demise.

abandonment of the wife; and the remainder brought in the last bride an average of 34 years prior to demise.[g]

Clearly, many demising families failed to renew themselves biologically. No doubt poverty made it difficult to attract and hold brides, but in a number of cases there was no person of marriageable age in the family owing to the prior departure of young people (daunted, perhaps, by the bleak prospect at home). Yet many landless families, equally badly off, as far as one can see, managed to keep marriageable sons or daughters at home and to survive. Part of the problem of demising families seems to have been a failure of affiliation.

Conclusions

In this chapter, we have seen that family size and composition varied directly with holding size, and that family size changed within a short time when holding size changed. We cannot say certainly from our data which way causation ran, that is, whether fam-

[g]Excluding seven cases in which the last marriage cannot be dated since it occurred before 1717, the year our record begins, and 13 cases in which the family head and husband of the last marriage died prematurely (before age 50). In families that did not demise the average length of time between marriages into the family was 34.6 years. Thus the timing of the demise of the last group of demising families came on average at about the time they would be expected to bring in brides.

ily change was typically a response to change in holding size or the cause of it. Probably it ran both ways to some extent. But in view of the critical importance of land to family survival and the ease of letting surplus land to others, it seems unlikely that families would normally sell land to adjust to family change. Family change in sympathy with changes in holding size through controlled exits and entries—especially exits—was probably the more usual mode of adjustment.

These exits and entries were voluntary for the family but not necessarily for the individual, for whom they could be painful, as when we find a daughter held within the family far beyond marriageable age (presumably for her labor), or a son in a large family sent off to work in his early teens.

The practice of making decisions on exits and entries of other kinds must have made the practice of infanticide somewhat easier. Both practices were adjustments of family size and membership for the presumed benefit of the family at the expense of individuals. Such decisions must frequently have been very difficult; that they occurred every generation in every family would have helped make them emotionally manageable and acceptable to others. So, too, would the conception of the family as a corporate entity with a life and interest that transcended those of its living members. To sacrifice those higher interests to the convenience of the moment—to sell off property handed down from the past in order to live comfortably in the present, for example—was reprehensible. To subordinate a momentary personal benefit to an enduring corporate interest was praiseworthy.

We do not suggest that all Nakahara families adjusted their size in the same ways or with equal success. Not all families practiced infanticide, since not all had occasion to; and some who did have reasons may have chosen not to. Nor was family adjustment always enough to cope with the external events affecting farming. Some demising families, through bad luck or bad management, seem to have reached a state in which they were powerless to adjust. They could not hold needed members, bring in new ones, or reproduce biologically. If success in farming depended substantially on the ability to adjust family membership shrewdly and consistently to farming needs, then to some extent the families that survived would be the successful adjusters. Rules of thumb about family size and the appropriate means of adjustment may have gotten established and handed down in these families in much the same way as farming skills. Families that neglected or shunned such rules may not have survived long enough to establish counter-traditions.

Chapter Eight   Marriage and the Family

WE HAVE ARGUED that Nakahara peasant families altered their size and composition in the interests of better farming, and especially in order to moderate the unfortunate effects of their own family cycle. This needs detailed illustration. Let us therefore consider marriage, which was both a part of the family cycle and, since its timing was variable, potentially a means of controlling cyclical effects. But first something must be said about the relation of marriage to inheritance.

Marriage and Inheritance

A marriage in normally occurred only once in a generation, since usually only the son intended as the next family head was allowed to bring in a bride. Sixty-five percent of males who married for the first time in Nakahara succeeded to the family headship, and another 8 percent who probably would have succeeded died or passed out of observation before they had the chance. The remaining 28 percent who married founded branch families. Only one male married and lived to age 50 without becoming a family head (see p. 90).

As for the sons and daughters who did not marry and stay in the family, nearly all who were old enough left shortly before or after the heir's marriage. About one in four sons were adopted out as husbands of daughters in families without male heirs, a common family predicament; the others either left the family and the village to work or disappeared from the record for unknown reasons (and thus had either died or migrated). Nearly all daughters were married out of the family. Fifteen apparently left for other reasons, but 12 of these departed in years of no record, or gap years, and so in all probability also married out. Of the remaining three, two left the village permanently for work, and one transferred to a branch family.

Practice was thus remarkably consistent—with only the heir remaining in the family and the other sons and daughters leaving—which suggests that the arrangement must have had important advantages. One such advantage, unquestionably, was to keep the family farm and other property intact from one generation to the next, assuring as nearly as possible that the family would continue in the village—and family survival was an overriding group aim. Rarely were holdings partitioned, and then usually only holdings large enough to be divided without danger to the main line; and even such holdings were divided very unequally (see Chapter 7). Had more than one son stayed home and married, this rule of impartible inheritance would have been difficult to enforce, since after the father's death the pressure to divide the property would have been intense. Indeed, in most cases where a second son married and stayed in the family, partitioning resulted soon after.[a]

There were other advantages to the dominant practice. Houses were small, and the departure of an heir's brothers and sisters created some living space and privacy for the new couple. It allowed the brother who could not stay permanently to leave at an age when, through apprenticeship or service to an employer, he might establish himself elsewhere in life and eventually marry. Also, since it was not always certain which brother was to inherit until a marriage in had occurred, the quick departure of the others may have been partly a way of avoiding bitterness in the family after the parents' choice became known.

But the inheritance system had the disadvantage of suddenly imposing a number of adverse changes on the family. Either just before or just after the marriage in, the groom typically became family

---

[a] Of course, causation may have run the other way, and the second son may have married because there was already willingness to divide. But the point remains that second and third sons usually left the family in order to prevent a division.

head, and there was always danger that he would be unable to establish his authority quickly and smoothly, or to use it wisely. The bride, who usually came from outside Nakahara,[b] was likely to cause discord between her husband and his mother, as well as between the mother and herself; and her untested ability as a worker in the family was nearly always something of a risk. In any case, her value as a worker would be limited for some time by childbearing, and the children would for many years be primarily consumers. Finally, at a time when dependents were being added to the family and the old folks were ceasing to be assets, the group was forced to give up all but one of its young adults, at the peak of their physical powers.

In Figure 8.1 can be seen the quantitative effect of this complex and dangerous transition in the life of families. All families with marriage in have been put on a common time-scale extending from nine years before marriage (M) to nine years after, and mean family size is graphed during this interval.[c] One sees the steep decline before marriage, the result of sons' and daughters' departures; there is a sharp but partial recovery with the entry of the bride; and after that there is steady expansion as children are born, eventually leading to a size above starting level, despite the departure of additional sons and daughters (and often the death of parents).

Consider the impact of these changes on farming capabilities. A group of adults (parents with grown children) is transformed by a single event into a group consisting of a single prime-aged male, a young and encumbered female, young children, and aging parents. A high ratio of workers to consumers becomes a low ratio. A low probability of loss to the group through death turns into an extraordinarily high one. And all of this at a time when the power of decision in the family is passing into new and inexperienced hands.

We can observe the nature of this transition more clearly by graphing the mean number of working members of the family dur-

---

[b] Of brides marrying Nakahara grooms for whom it was the first marriage, 73 percent came from outside the village.

[c] Families with more than one marriage in within the period have been eliminated from the sample.

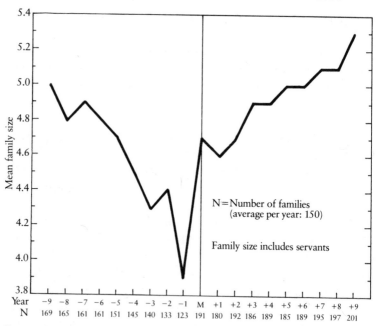

Fig. 8.1. Average size of families with marriages in, relative to the time of marriages

ing the nine years before and after marriage. The top line (with the scale on the left) of Figure 8.2 shows the average working capacity of the family as a whole, counting members under 20 and over 55 as various fractions of a full worker and mothers with children under 5 as one-half a worker.[d] Minor irregularities in the curve are apparently due to random variation with small numbers and can be overlooked. Except for the momentary increase at M owing to the bride's entry, the average family labor force declined steadily from six years prior to the marriage until nine years after, at which time it was about two-thirds starting size and still shrinking. The lower line (scale on right) graphs change in the most effective part of the

[d]Labor units at various ages (all JA) were calculated as follows, with no adjustment for sex except that used for mothers with young children. Aged 1–10: no labor units. Aged 11–19: add 0.1 labor unit for each year. Aged 20–55: 1.0 labor unit per person. Aged 56–65: subtract 0.1 unit for every two years past 55, to reach 0.5 at ages 64 and 65. Aged 66–69: subtract 0.1 unit for each year past 65, to reach 0 at age 70. Over 70: no units.

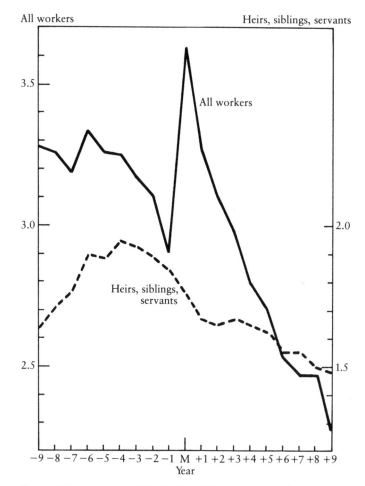

Fig. 8.2. Workers per family in families with marriages in, relative to the time of marriages

labor force, that is, the heir (or groom), his siblings, and the family servants. The curve of this group rose during the first five years of observation as the heir's siblings reached working age while remaining in the family. Then it fell, at first abruptly as siblings departed in anticipation of the marriage, and then more slowly after the marriage, since most siblings had gone by then.

Crisis is not too strong a term for the situation described by these curves. The size and quality of the family labor force declined drastically and did not begin to recover for a decade or more; and so small an absolute size was reached that the loss of a single worker through death or accident could bring a family to demise. Meanwhile, overall family size was steadily expanding. For ten years after the marriage, then, the family's working capacity and consumption needs were moving sharply in different directions.

There were two things a family could do to reduce the risks of this period. One was to postpone the marriage in as long as possible, thus prolonging the prior phase of maximum family strength, during which resources could be accumulated for the period to follow. The other was to retain noninheriting sons and daughters until the marriage in rather than releasing them as they came of age or wished to leave. These two maneuvers had to go together to be effective, of course. There was no point in postponing the marriage after noninheriting sons and daughters had left, and adult sons and daughters could be retained in the family only so long as it was postponed.

The gains from postponement, when this dual strategy was followed, were potentially great. Assuming that the marriage in would otherwise take place when the groom reached puberty, postponement could be eight to ten years or more. Thus a family's peak farming efficiency, attained when the children reached working age, could be realized for a decade or more, instead of entering immediately on decline. But there were also limits to postponement. The older the heir at marriage, the greater the danger that he would not live to raise his children; in that event, it might be impossible to recall a brother to the family to replace him, since the brothers would also be older and more likely to be committed to another course elsewhere (in a fair number of cases, there was no brother). At a certain point, then, the risk of further postponement would outweigh possible gains.

We can see how risk increased with postponement by consulting the life tables in Chapter 4 and making certain assumptions. Let us suppose that the prospective heir was age 20 and could marry whenever the family wished, and that a son would be born to him five years after marriage. We can then estimate his chances, at various ages at marriage, of living until the son in turn reached age 20, thus removing the danger that the father's death would leave the family without an adult male. The probabilities are as follows:

	Age at marriage					
	20	25	30	35	40	45
Chance of survival to son's age 20	0.79	0.73	0.65	0.58	0.53	0.41

We do not, of course, suggest that Nakaharans had a precise understanding of these odds; but they almost certainly knew that the risk in delaying marriage increased with age. And, perhaps as a compromise between the benefits and the dangers of delay, heirs' marriages in fact tended to take place in the late twenties (Table 8.1), with a modal age of 27.5 and a mean of 26.5.

Another possible explanation that comes to mind is that an heir's marriage was often delayed until his father died or retired as family head. But when we classify heirs by age at inheritance and calculate the mean age at first marriage for the various groups, no close connection between age at succession and age at marriage appears (Table 8.2). The timing of the heir's marriage, therefore, though influenced by the father's death or retirement, would seem to have been determined largely by other factors.

If an heir's marriage was delayed partly in order to postpone the reorganization of the family labor force, the decision need not have been closely reasoned, as opposed to rule-of-thumb. But perhaps one should not rule out too quickly all possibility of conscious planning. Farmers were used to planting early, medium, and late varieties of rice in order to stagger the work of the harvest; they knew precisely the cost of a day's labor; and they knew approxi-

TABLE 8.1

Heirs by Age at First Marriage

Groom's age	N	Percent	Groom's age	N	Percent
15–18	4	5%	27–30	26	32%
19–22	18	22	31–34	6	7
23–26	22	27	35 or more	6	7

NOTE: Includes all grooms except eight who subsequently left the family to found branches or to leave the village; included was one only child who died before inheriting.

TABLE 8.2

Heirs' Mean Age at First Marriage by Age at Inheritance

Age at inheritance	N	Mean age at marriage	Age at inheritance	N	Mean age at marriage
19 or less	10	24.2	30–34	28	28.3
20–24	15	24.8	35–39	8	25.8
25–29	11	25.7	40 or more	9	32.6

mately the number of man-days of work that each major farming operation required. Surely they were likewise capable of judging the advantages of postponing marriage in and the dangers of too long a postponement.

We are not dealing with people whose every action was guided by custom, though much has been written to that effect. Tokugawa books on agriculture, for the most part written by farmers for farmers, reveal men who were forever comparing crops, plant varieties, tools, and fertilizers for their practical effect on labor, costs, and yields.[1] These writers were a farming elite, no doubt, but one with a profound influence on ordinary peasants who competed to stay alive as farmers and as families. It does not seem too much to suppose that some of the shrewdness characteristic of farming was present in the farm family's conduct of its own affairs, especially as its affairs concerned farming.

Sons' Departures

We noted earlier that the value of postponing marriages in was contingent on keeping noninheriting sons and daughters in the family in the meantime. But it would be unreasonable to suppose that all sons and daughters would be released at the same time in any case, since they were of different ages. How, then, are we to tell whether they were deliberately retained or not? If departures tended to concentrate around the marriage in, we may infer that a conscious retention policy was in effect; if not, some other principle may have controlled them, such as departure at a conventional age or at will. We controlled for persons at risk by calculating the number of departures per year relative to the number of never-married sons and daughters (separately) aged 15 to 45 in the family.

Again, we arranged all families with a marriage in on a common time scale extending nine years on each side of the marriage (M), and then calculated for each year the departure rates per 1,000 persons at risk of sons and daughters. The nine-year observation period before and after marriage in was arbitrarily chosen, seeming long enough to catch most departures, and about as long as one could hope to perceive the influence of the marriage.

If a hold-and-release policy was generally in effect during this time, we would expect the departure rate to rise as the year of marriage approached and to fall following it. Any postponement (prior to M) would lower the rate in earlier years and raise it in a later one, and any hastening of departures (after M) would reduce the rate in a later year and raise it in an earlier one. The result of these two tendencies together must be a rising rate up to M and a falling rate after.

We found this tendency in Nakahara for sons' departures, though with considerable random fluctuation from year to year caused by the small numbers.[2] In order to smooth out the variations, we combined adjacent years to form five periods of three years each and a sixth period of four years. Figure 8.3 shows the results of the analysis using these periods. The departure rate rose from 20 in the first period to nearly 150 just before the marriage in, and then dropped steeply and continuously.

We see no possible explanation of this pattern except a conscious policy of retaining sons in the family. This can be further tested. Such a policy would require that older brothers of the groom leave

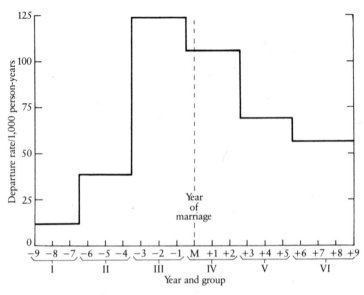

Fig. 8.3. Departure of unmarried sons, relative to the timing of marriages into the family (sons' departures per 1,000 sons aged 15–45)

the family at age on average older than younger brothers, and also that both older and younger brothers leave at ages on average older when the groom married late than when he married early. By contrast, departures at a conventional age, or at will, would contradict our supposition. In the event, we found that older brothers did stay

TABLE 8.3

Mean Age of Older and Younger Brothers at Departure,
According to Heir's Age at Marriage

Group	Heir's age at marriage		
	15–22	23–27	28–37
Younger brothers	16.9 (N = 8)	20.7 (N = 12)	22.8 (N = 13)
Older brothers	29.5 (N = 4)	36.5 (N = 1)	31.8 (N = 4)

NOTE: Confined to permanent departures during the −9 to +9 interval.

more than 10 years longer than younger brothers, on the average; and both older and (especially) younger brothers stayed longer when the heir married relatively late (Table 8.3).

Daughters' Marriages Out

The retention policy must have been more difficult to apply to daughters than to sons. Since sons generally left home to work outside Nakahara, there would be little to interfere with the postponement of their departure for a few years, except possibly a son's restlessness. But nearly all daughters left for marriage, and many things had to be taken into account in timing the event. Too long a postponement could make a girl unmarriageable, or could result in an unwelcome pregnancy. Marriage was a complicated matter to arrange; therefore, negotiations had to be begun well in advance, and once under way could not easily be halted. Also, marriage called for much hospitality and gift-giving, which were easier to manage in good crop years than in bad. Consequently, when the year was a good one and the girl was the right age, with the prospect of a desirable match, parents were not inclined to wait. There is evidence of this in the high marriage rate for years of low agricultural prices (i.e. abundant food supply; see p. 84).

Nevertheless, daughters' marriages out, like sons' departures, cluster around the heir's marriage in. The marriage rate per 1,000 for daughters in the five years before and after the marriage in (as a single period) was three times as high as the marriage rate for single females in all other years (186 vs. 56).[3] Also, as Figure 8.4 shows, the marriage rate for daughters, grouped by the six periods previously used for sons, rises before M and falls after it, though with two minor variations from the pattern of sons' departures.[4] Daughters' marriages peak one period later than sons' departures, and the marriage rate rises after an initial fall from period I to period II. The initial dip is probably a sampling error, but the displacement of the peak to the right seems to reflect a real difference between the timing of sons' and daughters' departures: sons tended to be released prior to M, and daughters at or after it. Could the

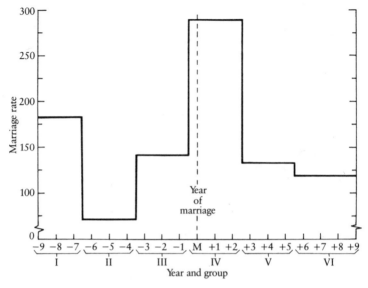

Fig. 8.4. Marriages out of daughters, relative to the timing of marriages into the family (marriages out per 1,000 daughters aged 15–45)

earlier release of sons have been because of hard feelings over the inheritance, or possibly to avoid sexual rivalry between brothers after the entry of a bride?

Another factor that had a significant influence on the timing of a daughter's marriage was the size of her family. Daughters in the five marriages out from families of two or three members married considerably older (mean age 22.5) than the twelve daughters marrying out of families of seven to ten members (mean age 17.3). The 42 daughters in medium-sized families of four to six members were intermediate between these ages (mean age 19.7). This progression probably existed because in a small family the daughter's presence was likely to be more critical than in a large one; she was likely to be the only adult female in the group, and the only person capable of performing the roles of cook, housekeeper, and surrogate mother.

We expected that daughters would be held longer in the families with large holdings, since the demand for farm labor in such families would be higher. Much to our surprise, the correlation ran strongly the other way. For the entire period 1716–1830, the larger the holding, the younger the ages of daughters at first marriage:

		Age at first marriage	
Holding size	N	Mean	Median
Small	42	22.6	22.5
Medium	48	20.4	19.5
Large	61	17.6	17.5

We had apparently forgotten two things that turned out to be important in this respect. First, because the letting of farm land was so prevalent, many small holders worked substantially more land than they held in title, and some large holders worked substantially less. Second, the families of small holders, as we saw in Chapter 7, tended to be decidedly smaller than those of large holders, with the result that daughters were probably more critical to their functioning. But whatever the linkage of marriage age to holding size and family size, it seems clear that family interest was the decisive factor in determining the timing of daughters' marriages.

Conclusions

Marriage in Nakahara showed a tendency for peasant families to adjust their size and composition to the requirements of farming. The family's phase of maximum farming efficiency was prolonged by postponing the heir's marriage as long as possible, and by detaining other children in the family in the meantime. Postponement is evident in the distribution of marriage ages for heirs, and detention in the rising rate of departure of the other children up to the heir's marriage, as well as the declining rate after. The policy need not have been conscious, but it is our personal opinion that it was so in some degree. There is a great deal of room between the extremes of rationality and perfect social conditioning; and the rationality of strictly farming decisions, which was evident in parts of Tokugawa Japan, would hardly have been wholly lacking in the management of the farm labor force, where laxness was likely to have the most serious consequences.

What was good for the family was obviously not always good for all its members. This is most obvious in the case of sons not picked as heir, who were held at home to work until a brother inherited, or was about to, and then sent off with little or no help to make a life as best they could elsewhere. This was not a case of individuals subordinating themselves to a common good in which they shared, since the noninheriting sons were excluded from the ultimate good done the family. How families were able to condition young males to comply with this system is not obvious. And they were not always successful in doing so; not infrequently adult members occupying a particularly disadvantaged position in the family slipped away without explanation, and probably in most cases they were fleeing a situation beneficial to others and without promise to themselves. But it would be a mistake to think that noninheriting sons were invariably family victims; in the poorest families the son who was ultimately free to leave may well have been better off than the son required to stay.

What happened to departing sons is a mystery,[e] except that they almost never returned. From the viewpoint of the village and its families these departures were beneficial. They relieved the village and its families of the burden of excess population, kept the unwanted population from reproducing in the village, and helped preserve the dominant system of single-son inheritance. Nakahara was not peculiar in this respect. Villages with a similar inheritance system and severe limits on the expansion of arable land were very common, and each year witnessed a vast exodus of young, unmarried males from these places. Where they went, how they were absorbed into the economy, whether they married or remained bachelors, whether they died according to the same pattern as other males, and above all whether important changes occurred in their numbers and typical fates during the eighteenth century are questions of great significance for Tokugawa social history.

[e] Except for sons who were adopted out. There were 24 such cases recorded for Nakahara families, most of the sons going to other villages. Since nearly all the adoptees were late adolescents or younger men, it seems likely that they were adopted as heirs by families without male issue.

Chapter Nine   Conclusion

Both mortality and fertility (adjusted for the late registration of infants) were low to moderate in Nakahara as compared
to eighteenth-century European rural parishes. We are almost
wholly in the dark about the causes of low mortality, but there can
be little doubt that one of the reasons for low registered fertility was
the practice of infanticide. This comes as no great surprise, given
the literary and legal evidence for infanticide in Tokugawa Japan.
What is surprising is that the practice does not appear to have been
primarily a response to poverty: large landholders practiced it as
well as small, and registered births were as numerous in bad as in
good growing years. Also, infanticide seems to have been used to
control the sex sequence and spacing of births and the sexual composition and final size of families. In short, it gives the impression of
a kind of family planning.

The phrase has an anachronistic ring. We are accustomed to
think of this kind of foresight as peculiarly modern, though there is
no obvious reason that it should be, given the necessary knowledge
of means and freedom from prejudice in using them. What is then
required is a lively appreciation of the relation of the size and composition of the family to its welfare; and this idea does not seem
intrinsically more difficult for premodern people to grasp than the
notion that improvements in agriculture required long-term effort.
In any case, there seems to have been no difficulty about this in
Nakahara, where the family and farming unit were indistinguish-
able, where decisions concerning one required decisions about the
other, and where farming was intensely competitive and perpetua-

tion of the family a religious duty. In saying this, we do not mean that all families practiced infanticide or practiced it in the same way; but enough did to give rise to the overall pattern of sex selection we find.

Obviously, we cannot extrapolate from the character of infanticide in Nakahara—one of tens of thousands of Tokugawa villages—to its character in the country, though there are very general reasons for thinking it may not have been greatly different elsewhere. For one thing, family farming was the rule over much or most of the country; and the survival of the family was commonly thought to be very much more important than the welfare of any one of its members, especially, one may suppose, a newborn baby not yet presented at the local shrine and thus not really a social being. Moreover, if infanticide was widely accepted as a means of fertility control, it would inevitably have been sex-selective, and so would have required the long-term consideration of sex balancing and sequence.

Beyond this, however, we have nationwide numerical data. Though by no means unambiguous, these are consistent with the supposition of a widespread use of infanticide as a means of planning. To state the case simply, there was a significant nationwide fall in the sex ratio during the eighteenth century that can be most convincingly accounted for as a shift in the sex incidence of infanticide, reflecting the increased economic value of women as a result of the growth of secondary and tertiary employment.

Table 9.1 shows the national sex ratio at eleven census dates in the Tokugawa period and at the Meiji registration of 1872. The ratio was an abnormally high 115 in 1732, the earliest census at which population by sex is known; thereafter it declined at every census but one until 1872, when it reached a more normal 103. Since there had been neither warfare nor migration into or out of the country for a century before 1732, the initially high sex ratio must have been a function of (1) female underregistration, (2) differential female mortality, or (3) infanticide practiced especially against females owing to their lesser value as workers and descendants.

TABLE 9.1
Sex Ratio of the Japanese Population, 1732–1872

Date	Sex ratio	Date	Sex ratio	Date	Sex ratio
1732	115.1	1786	111.6	1828	108.6
1750	114.2	1798	110.3	1834	108.0
1756	113.1	1804	110.1	1846	106.1
1762	113.6	1822	109.3	1872	103.0

SOURCE: Sekiyama, p. 267.

First, if females were underregistered in 1732, a gradual increase in their registration rate would account for the steady fall of the sex ratio thereafter. But there are two objections to this hypothesis. For one thing, scholars who have worked extensively with local population registers covering the whole of the eighteenth century and beyond have not gained the impression that registration improved with time; indeed, it may have deteriorated somewhat, which would not be surprising in view of the political decline of the regime after about 1780. Moreover, if the sex ratio declined through improved female registration, there should be a correlation in the provincial data between decline in sex ratio and population increase, and provinces with a large decline in the sex ratio ought to show relatively large population gains. But, unaccountably, the correlation runs the other way: the less the provincial decline in sex ratio, the greater the gain in population tended to be.[a]

Another explanation for the high sex ratio in 1732 would be high female mortality. In an agricultural and patrilineal society, it would not be surprising, if, aside from any sex bias in infanticide, female mortality was higher than male simply as the result of neglect and poor treatment. This alone could have produced the imbalance in the national sex ratio for 1732, and might also have created a tendency, which the data hint at, for the imbalance to be greatest in the

[a] The only two dates for which we can calculate sex ratio by province are 1750 and 1846. The correlation between sex ratios 1846/1750 and population 1846/1750 is +0.31, excluding Hokkaido. If we restrict the sample to the 19 provinces with exceptionally high sex ratios (116 or over) in 1750, the correlation still obtains but declines to +0.22.

economically most backward provinces and least in the most commercial. In this case, the decline in the sex ratio after 1732 could have resulted from an improvement in female mortality relative to male, possibly as a consequence of the changing economy. With the mortality data now available it is impossible to examine this possibility closely, but it clearly cannot be excluded.[b]

Finally, if the high sex ratio in 1732 was the result mainly of female infanticide, its subsequent fall could have come about in two ways. First, the outright abandonment of the practice of infanticide would in time have produced a more normal sex ratio. The difficulty here is that we can think of no convincing reason why infanticide, which must have served an important social purpose, should have been abandoned. Moralists and the government had always condemned it with no noticeable effect. And although government efforts to suppress the practice became more conspicuous with time, so did the government's inability to override peasants' interests in the villages—as is evident in the various attempts to regulate rural trade and industry.[c] It has been suggested that infanticide may have been replaced by abortion; but again, it is not clear

[b] Our data for Nakahara show female mortality throughout the whole period of study as distinctly lower than male; also, the female advantage was greatest in the earliest of the four periods used in analyzing mortality (see page 000). On the other hand, Hayami found that female life expectancy in Yokouchi improved from 79 percent of male life expectancy in the period 1671–1725 to 103 percent in the period 1726–75. But since there was a large increase in the long-distance migration of males for work during the second period in Yokouchi, the relative improvement in female mortality may have been in part the result of the relative depletion of the most vigorous males in the 20–40 age group. Hayami, *Kinsei nōson*, pp. 166, 204.

[c] Increasingly, after the mid-eighteenth century, the Tokugawa government attempted to confine the sale of certain staples to licensed wholesalers, who paid for their monopolies in "thank money" (*reikin*) and taxes. These monopolies proved difficult to enforce in the countryside, though less so in the towns. The merchant guilds that aided enforcement in the towns had less power in rural areas, and the obstacles to surveillance presented by space and terrain were great. Enforcement was largely in the hands of village authorities, since for a century or more *samurai* had been removed from most of the countryside and concentrated in castle towns. The result was to place day-to-day responsibility in the hands of solitary village communities, who, in this and in some other matters, had a strong interest in noncompliance. See Smith, "Urbanization and Premodern Economic Growth," pp. 144–45.

why such a substitution would take place. Infanticide is sex-selective, less dangerous to the mother, simpler in technical requirements, and actually more efficient in controlling fertility owing to the much longer period of sterility associated with a full-term pregnancy. Thus the practice would seem unquestionably superior to abortion on all but moral grounds. (Neither moralists nor government, however, made any distinction between the two. Rather, they condemned both absolutely as contrary to the laws of man and nature.)

If infanticide was not completely abandoned, there could still have been a drop in the sex ratio if there were a long-term shift favorable to females in the sex incidence of infanticide. In Nakahara, where the sex ratio at registered birth was 114, or almost identical to the national sex ratio in 1732, infanticide was nevertheless apparently practiced almost equally against males and females. Whether a male or female child was preferred in a particular case appears to have depended largely on the sex balance of the previous and still-living children of the parents. Thus there were often occasions on which girls were accepted and boys rejected. Now assume for the moment that this was the case in the country as a whole in 1732, and that later there was a gradual increase in the economic value of females relative to males. Surely the change would have been reflected in the practice of infanticide. No change in moral outlook would have been required, only a marginal shift in sex bias in response to changed economic conditions. This would have lowered the sex ratio without increasing population (unless, of course, it was accompanied by a desire for larger families).

But what could have raised the general valuation of females relative to males? Two well-documented economic developments together may have had this effect.

One was the increasing difficulty of partitioning holdings between sons, which resulted from the drastic slowing of the rate of land reclamation in the latter half of the Tokugawa period. Local studies of individual villages have repeatedly shown a decrease in the average size of holdings during the eighteenth century, and a concurrent decline in the frequency of partitioning.[d] In the circumstances suggested by these trends—it must usually have been impossible to partition without danger to the family—there might have been a tendency to look more favorably on girl babies, who presented no danger of future pressure to partition. Females were not normally potential heirs if there were sons, though they could inherit and provide heirs (through marriage in) if sons died. They also could be married out, whereas there was no equally reliable way of establishing noninheriting sons outside the family. And within the family daughters were nearly as useful as sons; besides helping with domestic chores, they could work in the fields or be sent off before marriage to work for wages. An increase in the proportion of practically impartible holdings, therefore, might have led to some substitution of daughters for sons and a consequent lowering of the sex ratio at birth.

The other development that might have changed the status of females was the growth of trade and industry, which occurred in some degree nearly everywhere in Japan and transformed the economies of some regions, especially rural areas. One effect of this was almost certainly to increase the ratio of female to male employment. Sericulture, tea processing, textiles, papermaking, and of course service occupations—work in eating places, grog shops, roadside stands, inns, or brothels—were wholly or predominantly female employments.[e] Some of these occupations women could fol-

---

[d] An example is the village of Machinota in Tamba Province, studied by Miyakawa Mitsuru. The number of families in the village increased from 7 in 1658, to 17 in 1712, 29 in 1807, and 32 in 1869. The modal size of holdings declined from 5–10 *koku* in 1674 to 1–3 *koku* in 1815, and to 1 *koku* or less in 1869. Between 1658 and 1735, one in three inheritances entailed a partitioning of the holding, whereas the corresponding figure for the period 1735–1869 was one in ten. Miyakawa, pp. 52, 62.

[e] One of the most famous Tokugawa books on sericulture, *Yōsan suchi* (1794), laments the prejudice of male farmers against caring for silkworms and their consequent ignorance of the subject; women, by contrast, were occupied in sericulture from childhood. The author thought this an obstacle to the best results: "Although there are naturally intelligent women, their understanding is inferior to that of a stupid man, and as a result [in raising silkworms] they are unable to adjust their methods to unexpected changes in the weather." (*Yōsan suchi* ms. in National Diet Library, I, 11.)

low at home; others they left home to work at. If Mark Fruin's data from the Echizen villages that he has studied are representative, women in rural areas left home for work almost as commonly as men, though they traveled shorter distances.[1] At the same time, the expansion of nonagricultural male employment, by permitting more noninheriting sons to marry, may have increased the demand for wives.

If the economic value of women relative to men increased as a result of these developments, we might expect the sex incidence of infanticide to have shifted in favor of females, which would also have tended to alleviate the pressure on families to partition. No massive shift would have been required to bring the sex ratio down from 115 to normal over a period of a century and a half.

All this speculation is susceptible to a limited measure of testing, using two sets of data that permit us to discover whether there was a negative correlation between sex ratio and the development of trade and industry in different localities. Was it the case that the more these nonagricultural sectors grew, the lower the sex ratio tended to be? Such a relationship, which might have several causes, would not prove our case; but it would be consistent with our hypotheses, whereas the absence of the relationship would tend to discredit them.

One set of data comes from Chōshū, the large two-province fief at the southern end of Honshū. In 1843, the fief government conducted the most detailed economic survey made anywhere in the Tokugawa period, requiring its administrative districts—each containing a score or more of villages and a total population of several thousand—to complete a long and detailed questionnaire. The completed survey itemized for each district the output and the costs of production in an "average" year, including products consumed at home, gave the value of nearly all of the items in current prices, and reported population by sex, occupation, and tax category. From these returns we were able to calculate for 57 districts the share of income by economic sector—primary (agriculture, fishing, and lumbering), secondary (handicraft and manufacturing), and tertiary (trade, transport, and services)—and to correlate these values with sex ratio and per capita income. Table 9.2 summarizes the results.[f]

Per capita income was correlated negatively with the income share of the primary sector, not at all with that of the secondary sector, and positively with that of the tertiary sector. In other words, per capita income tended to be higher the more commercial and the less agricultural the economy of a district became, and to be little affected by the level of handicrafts and manufacturing. Sex ratio was negatively correlated with both per capita income and the income share of the tertiary sector, and positively but slightly with the income share of the primary and secondary sectors. That is, the higher the per capita income and the more commercial the economy, the lower the sex ratio; the lower the per capita income and the more agricultural the economy, the higher the sex ratio.

We cannot be sure that these relationships represent a course of historical development—that in any given district the sex ratio tended to fall over time as the tertiary sector and per capita income expanded. Also, even assuming this to be the case, the sex ratio could have been reduced either by a shift in the sex bias of infanticide or by females leaving some districts and entering others in larger numbers than males. However, this would not be true of the declining sex ratio nationwide, which could have occurred in several ways already discussed but not through migration, since there was no movement in or out of the country during nearly the whole period of the decline. Also, any fall in local sex ratios in response to commercialization, whether by migration or infanticide, would

[f]The values cited in the questionnaire returns of different districts purport to be either three-year averages or a mean struck between good and bad years by unspecified calculations. We used local prices in calculating income in all cases where they were given; for the few items not priced locally, we used prices from neighboring districts or, when these were not available, Osaka prices for 1843. The districts involved came from three administrative jurisdictions—Kaminoseki, Mitajiri, and Mine—which were chosen for study because they were large, had varied economies and topographies, and itemized output and production costs in greater detail and with more clarity than other districts. For further discussion of the sources and an analysis of by-employments and trade flows in Kaminoseki, see Smith, "Farm Family By-Employments in Preindustrial Japan."

TABLE 9.2
Correlation of Sex Ratio and Various Economic Indicators for Chōshū in 1843

Indicator	Sex ratio	Share of primary sector	Share of secondary sector	Share of tertiary sector	Per capita primary income	Per capita secondary income	Per capita tertiary income	Per capita total income
Sex ratio	1.00	0.19	0.10	−0.37	−0.16	−0.13	−0.37	−0.39
Share of primary sector		1.00	−0.72	−0.70	0.77	−0.66	−0.67	−0.31
Share of secondary sector			1.00	0.01	−0.66	0.67	0.11	0.05
Share of tertiary sector				1.00	−0.43	−0.26	0.86	0.39
Per capita primary income					1.00	−0.36	−0.34	0.22
Per capita secondary income						1.00	0.59	0.73
Per capita tertiary income							1.00	0.73
Per capita total income								1.00

suggest a rise in the relative value of female labor, which ought to be reflected in some change in the sex bias of infanticide.

Our second set of data, compiled by Professor Hayami from an unpublished government document of 1875, shows the percentage of population living in towns of 5,000 or more at that date for each of fourteen regions of the country.[2] These figures can be matched with the provincial population figures for 1846, the last Tokugawa census,[g] to see whether there is any correlation between regional urbanization—as a rough indicator of the level of development of tertiary industry—and regional sex ratio (1846). Remember that

[g] To the best of our knowledge, figures on provincial population *by sex* are not available for the Meiji registration of 1872.

between these dates the Tokugawa pattern of urbanization had begun to change owing to the opening of the country to foreign trade in 1858 and the establishment of the Meiji government in 1868. Nevertheless, we find almost the same correlation (-0.38) between these two measures as between sex ratio and the tertiary sector in Chōshū. In other words, the higher the level of urbanization, the lower the sex ratio; and the lower the level of urbanization, the higher the sex ratio. Again, the development of nonagricultural employments seems to be associated with a declining sex ratio.

All of this is far from proving that sex-selective infanticide and a kind of family planning were widely practiced in Tokugawa Japan, but it makes that hypothesis not altogether improbable. Given this, the time-consuming and painstaking testing of the possibility in the only way available—the analysis of suitable runs of population registers from other Tokugawa villages by methods similar to those used here—seems worthwhile. We might hope that this testing would lead to a better understanding of the relation of population growth to industrialization, of the possibility of family planning by preindustrial populations, and of the cultural and material factors influencing sex preferences in the practice of infanticide. On the other hand, we must remind the reader once again that such testing could easily reveal Nakahara as an ethnographic curiosity with no substantial parallel elsewhere in Japan.

Reference Matter

Appendix A   Nakahara's Population

Tables A.1 and A.2 summarize the data from which our estimates of mortality were derived. For the *de jure* population, as contrasted with the actual resident population referred to elsewhere in the text, we included persons working outside the village of whom there was a continuous year-to-year record during their absence. Such absentees contributed both person-years and deaths to the *de jure* data.

TABLE A.1

De Jure Population: Person-years, Birth Groups, and Immigrants

Standard age registered	DE JURE POPULATION								
	Person-Years			Birth groups (*by mother's age*)			Immigrants		
	F	M	T	F	M	T	F	M	T
0	308	354	662	0	0	0	0	0	0
1	1,111	1,265	2,376	0	0	0	3	4	7
5	1,187	1,401	2,588	0	0	0	5	2	7
10	1,105	1,290	2,395	0	1	1	10	9	19
15	1,037	1,179	2,216	25	23	48	102	13	115
20	999	1,089	2,088	76	74	150	46	15	61
25	861	1,013	1,874	69	85	154	19	17	36
30	761	917	1,678	61	79	140	10	10	20
35	683	855	1,538	42	55	97	7	4	11
40	638	767	1,405	26	20	46	1	4	5
45	601	664	1,265	4	8	12	2	1	3
50	540	565	1,104	1	2	3	1	1	2
55	489	470	958	1	0	1	0	0	0
60	438	414	852	0	0	0	1	0	1
65	370	343	712	0	0	0	1	0	1
70	254	216	470	0	0	0	0	0	0
75	143	143	286	0	0	0	0	0	0
80	84	62	146	0	0	0	0	0	0
85	51	40	90	0	0	0	0	0	0
TOTAL	11,656	13,042	24,698	309	355	664*	208	80	288

* Includes 12 "cause unknown" entries, 2 of which are at more than JA2.

TABLE A.2

Deaths, Emigrants, and Unexplained Departures

| Standard age registered | ALL PERSONS | | | | | | | | |
| | Deaths | | | Emigrants | | | Unexplained departures | | |
	F	M	T	F	M	T	F	M	T
0	2	1	3	0	2	2	0	0	0
1	31	50	81	2	3	5	1	1	2
5	11	12	23	2	1	3	2	3	5
10	8	10	18	16	8	24	4	6	10
15	7	9	16	72	9	81	5	4	9
20	9	11	20	45	9	54	3	9	12
25	6	8	14	26	8	34	5	10	15
30	6	9	15	13	7	20	6	4	10
35	7	7	14	9	4	13	2	1	3
40	3	14	17	2	9	11	0	3	3
45	8	13	21	3	3	6	0	3	3
50	12	12	24	2	4	6	0	0	0
55	9	12	21	0	1	1	0	0	0
60	9	9	18	2	0	2	0	0	0
65	14	20	34	0	1	1	0	0	0
70	25	18	43	1	1	2	0	0	0
75	13	14	27	0	0	0	0	0	0
80	13	12	25	0	0	0	0	0	0
85	9	7	16	0	0	0	0	0	0
TOTAL	202	248	450	195	70	265	28	44	72

Appendix B   Infant Mortality

The Nakahara life tables, when graphed (see Chapter 4), bore a strong resemblance to the Coale-Demeny model "North" series of life tables. This visual impression was confirmed by the following test. On the basis of the life expectation column (e_x) for age 1 and above from our life tables, we prepared a set of implied e_0 values according to each of the four regional Coale-Demeny models. The standard deviation within each set of implied values was used as a goodness-of-fit index, with the smallest deviation implying the best fit. The results are summarized in Table B.1. On balance, our low estimate of mortality (all 72 cause-unknown disappearances treated as migrations) gives a better fit than the medium or high estimates, and the pattern of mortality in our tables most resembles model "North."

As discussed in Chapter 2, however, we thought it necessary to make high and low estimates of infant mortality based on "East" and "North." Also, we projected each model back to age 0 using two methods: one employing the entire e_x column and the other age group 1−5 only (Table B.2). This gave two low and two high estimates for each sex as seen in Table B.1. In order to get a single figure, we averaged the lows and the highs separately and took their mean. Using these infants' death rates, we were able to estimate life expectancy at birth for our low, medium, and high life tables.

TABLE B.1
Standard Deviations of Implied e_0 in Nakahara, 1717−1830

Coale-Demeny population	Female			Male		
	Low	Medium	High	Low	Medium	High
West	2.99	3.93	5.06	4.06	5.43	6.94
North	2.25	3.12	4.28	2.70	4.06	5.63
East	3.52	4.51	5.66	4.39	5.75	7.22
South	3.25	4.06	5.09	4.16	5.45	6.90

TABLE B.2

Estimates of Nakahara Infant Mortality Based on De Jure
Population and Coale-Demeny Regional Model Life Tables

Period and group	Female		Male	
	Low (N)	High (E)	Low (N)	High (E)
Fitted on e_x column				
1800–1830	.09	.13	.13	.21
1775–99	.15	.24	.17	.25
1750–74	.09	.13	.13	.21
1717–49	.14	.20	.17	.28
1717–1830 overall	.12	.17	.15	.24
Landholding				
Over 12 *koku*	.11	.16	.10	.15
Under 12 *koku*	.14	.20	.17	.29
Total 1758–1800	.12	.17	.14	.21
Fitted on $_4q_1$ estimate				
1800–1830	.18	.29	.15	.25
1775–99	.13	.21	.15	.25
1750–74	.13	.22	.21	.35
1717–49	.03	.06	.26	.45
1717–1830 overall	.13	.21	.18	.32
Landholding				
Over 12 *koku*	.11	.18	.19	.33
Under 12 *koku*	.17	.28	.13	.23
Total 1758–1830	.13	.22	.17	.29

Appendix C   Land Transfers

1. For the total change in all holdings' size, add all plus or minus changes in individual holdings from one observation to the next. Note that this counts the same piece of land twice to the extent that land was transferred from one holding to another; thus it counts both land gained by holder A and land lost by holder A. Total change: 3,093,937 *koku*.

2. All plus or minus changes in *village* arable (total of all individual holdings) from one observation to the next are taken as the total amount of change through land being newly brought into and taken out of cultivation. Note that this will be an underestimate, since it reflects *net* change only. It takes no account (and none can be taken) of offsetting changes from the same arable going into and out of cultivation. Total: 313,635 *koku*.

3. Changes in individual holdings through partitioning can be closely estimated. They are two times the difference in the *koku* held by main families at the observation prior to partitioning and by branch families at the next observation. The figure is doubled to take account of the land lost by the main families as well as that gained by branches. Total: 778,640 *koku*.

4. Subtract the totals accumulated in 2 and 3 from the total in 1 to get the losses and gains in individual holdings that were the result of transfers of land between holders through sale or foreclosure. Total: 2,001,662 *koku*.

5. Since the totals for 3 and 4 count each transfer of land twice, once for the gainer and once for the loser, multiply each of these items by 0.5 in order to make the item as nearly as possible symmetrical with 2, which is a *net* figure. The figures thus become 389,320 *koku* for 3 and 1,000,831 *koku* for 4.

6. Total changes in individual holdings by source are then:

From changes in arable (2)	313,635 *koku*	18.41%
From partitioning (revised 3)	389,320	22.85
From transfers of land		
between holders (revised 4)	1,000,831	58.74
TOTAL	1,703,786 *koku*	100.00%

Notes

Chapter 1

1. R. H. Tawney, *Land and Labour in China*, p. 79.
2. Chaunu, *Histoire science sociale*, pp. 321–23.
3. Krause, "Some Neglected Factors in the English Industrial Revolution," pp. 104–5; Drake, *Population and Society in Norway*, p. 49; Chandrasekhar, *Asia's Population Problems*, p. 14.
4. Spengler, "Demographic Factors and Early Modern Economic Development," pp. 441–44.
5. See Hayami, "The Population at the Beginning of the Tokugawa Period," pp. 27 *et seq.*
6. Nakamura, "Hōken-teki tochi shoyū kaitai no chiiki-teki tokushitsu," pp. 130–32. Umemura, "Tokugawa jidai no jinkō sūsei," p. 138.
7. Umemura, pp. 137, 139.
8. *Ibid.*, p. 137; Hayami, "Tokugawa kōki jinkō hendō," pp. 67–68. Hayami believes that at the same time double counting may have decreased.
9. Umemura, p. 137; Hayami, "Tokugawa kōki jinkō hendō," p. 68; Hayami, "The Population at the Beginning of the Tokugawa Period," p. 4. However, Hanley and Yamamura, in "Population Trends and Economic Growth in Preindustrial Japan," p. 485, express more serious reservations about reliability.
10. Hayami, "Tokugawa kōki jinkō hendō," pp. 70–73.
11. For regional examples, see Katō, "Hansei ni okeru Owari no jinkō no bunpu to hendō," pp. 179–87; Hanley, "Population Trends and Economic Development"; Sekiyama, p. 249.
12. For a contemporary view, see Hoashi, "Tosenpuron," p. 221.
13. Perkins, *Agricultural Development in China*, p. 207.
14. Gille, "The Demographic History of the Northern Countries in the Eighteenth Century," p. 19.
15. Drake, *Population and Society in Norway*, p. 49. For other rates in

the eighteenth and nineteenth centuries, see Clark, *Population Growth and Land Use*, p. 64.

16. See Sekiyama, pp. 130–33.

17. Taeuber, *The Population of Japan*, p. 20. Taeuber also remarks (p. 21): "These are the types of fluctuations [from year to year] that might be expected in a population that had approached the limits of subsistence at the existing technical level, a population in which changes in food supply were reflected in fairly immediate and roughly compensatory adjustments in numbers."

18. See Aoki, pp. 10–11, 16–18; Horie, pp. 51–95. These are only two of many examples.

19. An interesting work of this kind is Nakamura, "Hōken-teki tochi shoyū kaitai no chiiki-teki tokushitsu." For convenient summaries of Japanese literature bearing on growth in the Tokugawa period, see Hanley and Yamamura, "A Quiet Transformation in Tokugawa Economic History"; Furushima, "Shōhin ryūtsū no hatten to ryōshu keizai." Additional citations appear in Smith, "Urbanization and Premodern Economic Growth," p. 154.

20. See Henry, *Manuel de démographie historique*, pp. 89–90. A bibliography of work in Japanese population history, almost all of it in Japanese, appears in Shakai keizai shi gakkai (ed.), pp. 219 *et seq.*

21. Crude rates are available for several towns, but no age-specific rates except a graph in Sasaki, "Hida no kuni Takayama no jinkō kenkyū," p. 116. This situation promises to be modified soon through Sasaki's work. Crude rates are found in this article and in the same author's "Tokugawa toshi jinkō no kenkyū."

22. This evidence is extensively reviewed in Takahashi, *Nihon jinkō-shi no kenkyū*.

23. The net loss of population through migration, however, was nothing special; it also occurred in 1701–25 and 1751–75, as well as in all periods after 1775 except 1851–71. Hayami, *Kinsei nōson*, pp. 160–61.

24. *Ibid.*, p. 218.

25. *Ibid.*

Chapter 2

1. Akimoto Motoya has used these same registers in two 1973 papers that deal in part with Nakahara: "Kinsei nōmin kazoku no kibo to keitai" and "Kinsei nōmin no kōdō kansatsu." His findings overlap ours only slightly.

2. See Umemura, "Tokugawa jidai no jinkō sūsei," pp. 134–46.

3. See Smith, "The Land Tax in the Tokugawa Period," pp. 263–83;

and "Urbanization and Premodern Economic Growth: Japan and the West," pp. 152–54.

4. Smith, "Land Tax," pp. 263–83.

Chapter 4

1. Our life tables were computed as follows: person-years of exposure to the risk of death were accumulated in appropriate age groups for all members of the population. For example, a person who moved to Nakahara at 23.5 years, stayed 18 years, and then died, would contribute 1.5 years to group 20–24, 5 years each to the next three groups, and 1.5 years to group 40–44; the death itself would be accumulated in the 40–44 age group. Deaths and person-years accumulated in this way were used to compute age-specific death rates $(_nm_x)$. The age-specific probabilities of death $(_nq_x)$ during the next five-year period were then computed by the formula:

$$_5q_x = \frac{5 \times {_5m_x}}{1 + 2.5 \times {_5m_x}}$$

This formula assumes that the average person-years lived by those who died in an interval equal half the length of the interval for ages below 5, an assumption not always tenable (see Chiang, *Introduction to Stochastic Processes in Biostatistics*, Chap. 9). We observed that for the total sample this number came to approximately 1.8 years, so that for age group 1–5

$$_4q_1 = \frac{4 \times {_4m_1}}{1 + 2.8 \times {_4m_1}}$$

2. See Preston, "Influence of Cause-of-Death Structure on Age-Patterns of Mortality."

3. Our major source of socioeconomic information, as noted in Chapter 2, is a series of ten listings of land assessments between 1716 and 1823 at intervals of approximately ten years. These give the assessed productivity (*kokudaka*) of each family's holding in *koku* of rice, including 0 for landless families. To keep the subsets of population as large as possible we were obliged to use only two categories, merging all ten observations to calculate the median between large and small holdings. In order to assign each person a holding size for each year of life, we (1) took the family's holding size in any given nonobservation year to be the same as its holding size in the closest observation year; (2) used the family's holding size in a given year as the holding size for each of its members; (3) altered the individual's holding size in the event of a change of family through marriage, adoption, or divorce; and (4) in the event of a change in holding size that entailed a

movement between classes of holders, attributed the person-years on either side of the median to the appropriate group.

Chapter 5

1. On the comparatively low levels of age-specific fertility in southwestern France, see Valmary, *Familles paysannes*, Chap. 6; Henry, "Fécondité des mariages," pp. 612–40, 977–1023, especially 985, 991, 1001–5; Goubert, "Legitimate Fecundity and Infant Mortality," pp. 593–603, especially 597–99.

2. It is standard practice to omit the 15–19 age group in computing total fertility, since inclusion of that group would introduce two serious biases: (1) adolescent sterility would greatly reduce the actual fertility of the 15–19 age group if all women married at 15, but in fact the rate attributed to the whole group is usually computed from a few women who marry at 18 or 19; (2) in many communities early marriers show an exceptionally high birth rate because of marriages forced by pregnancy.

3. Table based on Henry, *Manuel de démographie historique*, pp. 89–90; see also Wrigley, "Family Limitation," p. 91.

4. Henry, "Some Data on Natural Fertility," pp. 90–91.

5. The most comprehensive study of this sort of evidence is the massive work by Takahashi Bonsen, *Nihon jinkō-shi no kenkyū* [Studies of Japanese Population History].

6. We can test for homogeneity of the three groups by applying the χ^2 test to a 3×2 contingency table consisting of the distributions of the sex of the next child in the three groups; the null hypothesis is that births are independent of each other and of the composition of the existing sibling set. Four degrees of freedom are lost in our assumption that the true probability of a male birth equals the observed proportion of male births in the total sample (99/184 or 0.54), and that the expected frequency of births in each class of sibling composition equals the observed frequency. We get a χ^2 of 10.6, significant at the 0.006 level on two degrees of freedom. If the expected sex ratio at birth is 105, the expected sex ratio at age 1 (registered birth) would be 102 by model "North" of the Coale-Demeny life tables (which most closely resembles the Nakahara life tables for mortality at standard age 1 or older). We can test for sex bias in any distribution of sex by applying the χ^2 test on the null hypothesis that the true sex ratio at (registered) birth is 102. The results for the three groups are as follows:

Siblings	χ^2	Degrees of freedom	Level of significance
PM	3.4	1	0.07
M = F	1.9	1	0.17
PF	5.7	1	0.02

7. Applying the test for sex bias as described in note 6, we get the following figures for all first marriages:

Siblings	χ^2	Degrees of freedom	Level of significance
PM	3.6	1	0.06
M = F	3.8	1	0.05
PF	5.6	1	0.02

Applying the test for homogeneity as described in note 6, we get a χ^2 of 11.2, significant at the 0.004 level on two degrees of freedom.

8. We applied the χ^2 test to the 2 × 2 contingency table corresponding to all cases regardless of living sibship composition, using the null hypothesis that the sex of a deceased child was unrelated to the sex of the next child, and with two assumptions: (1) that the true probability of a male birth equals the observed frequency in the sample (0.49); and (2) that the expected frequencies of births in both classes of deceased child equal the observed frequencies. This yielded a highly significant χ^2 statistic of 10.7 (0.001 level) on one degree of freedom. Moreover, for both classes of deceased child, the sex ratio of the next birth deviates significantly (0.02 level) from 102.

9. Comparison with other countries is complicated by the fact that the median age of Nakahara women at first marriage was 18.5 years, about 5 years younger than the median in most Western European parishes. However, if we restrict ourselves to cases in which the wife was less than age 30 at the time of marriage, the mean family size for complete first marriages in Nakahara was 5.2 children, as compared with 6.1 children and 8.0 children for complete marriages in the French parishes of Crulai (1675–1744) and Meulan (1660–1739), respectively. (Calculated from figures in Gautier and Henry, *La Population de Crulai*, p. 126; Lachiver, *Meulan*, p. 171.) Only two complete first marriages in Nakahara (each producing three children) are eliminated because of this restriction.

10. The proportions for Meulan are computed from data in Lachiver, *Meulan*, pp. 171–72.

11. Testing for homogeneity, as in note 8, we get a χ^2 of 4.6, significant at the 0.10 level on two degrees of freedom.

12. First, for each family during its period of existence we construct a function of farming income in *kokudaka* over time, using straight-line interpolations between registration dates and horizontal interpolations forward and backward for the first and last dates, respectively. We then calculate for each completed first marriage the average annual income of the family over the time interval from the beginning of the marriage through the end of the wife's fecundity (age 45). Finally, we divide these marriages equally into landholding classes above and below the median.

13. For most demographic events in Nakahara we have only the year of the event's occurrence; as explained in Chapter 2, the assumption that births occur at midyear can be expected to entail an average error of no more than one month. A more serious source of error arises from our inability to account for unregistered births ("infant mortality"), which would add to the length of the birth intervals. Thus our birth intervals are less accurate than and not strictly comparable with conventionally measured intervals for which exact dates of birth are available. At first sight, the 0–1 interval in Nakahara looks suspiciously long as compared with the European norm of about 1.5 years or less. However, 70 percent of the brides in completed first marriages married before age 20, and 39 percent before age 18. And the mean first-birth interval decreases as age of marriage increases:

Age at marriage	Number of cases	Mean first-birth interval
16 or younger	15	3.4 yrs.
17–19	30	2.6
20 or older	19	1.9

Thus it seems probable that adolescent sterility, in conjunction with "infant mortality" and some infanticide, could well account for the length of the 0–1 birth interval.

14. See Langer, "Infanticide: A Historical Survey"; Kellum, "Infanticide in England in the Later Middle Ages"; Bergues et al., La Prévention des naissances dans la famille, especially Chap. 6, "Exposition, abandon d'enfants, infanticides." For Japan, see the works by Takahashi and Sekiyama.

Chapter 6

1. Hayami, "Jinkō gakuteki shihyō ni okeru kaisōkan no kakusa," p. 180.

2. In Rikuzen Province, Miyagi District: "If the wife is not harmonious with the husband, or does not please the parents-in-law, she may be divorced." In Musashi Province, Toshima District: "Sometimes, in spite of the fact that the husband and wife are on [sic] harmonious relations, the wife is divorced because she does not please her parents-in-law." Wigmore, Law and Justice, VII, 92–93.

3. For example, in Sagami Province, Kamakura District: "If the husband commits a crime, the wife's family has the right to demand a divorce, and if he refuses, his relatives and company men [of the five-family group] must stand as witnesses and divorce the wife. Once divorced, the husband has no right of protest if the wife remarries on the next day." In Kai Province, Yamanashi District: "If the husband ill-treats the wife, is dissolute, or commits a crime so that there is no possibility of the wife's continuing relations, the wife's family may demand a divorce." "Pressure of poverty

sometimes causes separation by mutual consent. . . ." Quotes similar to these might be greatly extended in number. *Ibid.*, pp. 90–95.

Chapter 7

1. Ōbata, "Saizōki," p. 411.
2. Quoted in Seki, *Hansei kaikaku*, p. 83.
3. Musumi Takehachi, "Zayū tekagami," p. 291.
4. Examples here are from documents in *Okuda ke monjo*, XI, 776–96.
5. The rate of family demise was calculated as 1,000 × (*D*/*Y*), where *D* is the number of families in the sample that went out of existence during the period of record and *Y* is the sum of the total number of years individual families were in existence in the village during the period of record, counting each family each year as 1. Of the 55 cases of founding of branch families, one case where the branch-family founder returned to the main family after three years is not included. Of the remaining 54 branch families, 17 died out during the period of record. Of the 36 main families from which these branches were founded (some, of course, founded more than one branch), eight had disappeared by 1830.
6. For example, see Smith, *The Agrarian Origins of Modern Japan*, Chapter 12.
7. Ōbata, "Saizōki," p. 411.
8. Nomura and Yoshii, p. 184.
9. "Yōsan kyōkō roku," in Inosaki, *Sansō kōten shūsei*, p. 411.
10. Ōkura, "Nōgu benri ron," pp. 100–101.
11. Nomura and Yoshii, p. 188.
12. Inosaki, p. 289.
13. Nomura and Yoshii, p. 208.
14. Ōbata, "Saizōki," p. 399.
15. Since a 10-percent change in holding size would have had a different impact on families with different sized holdings, we attempted to control for this factor by limiting consideration to families whose holdings did not fall below 14 *koku* (median size) or go above 50 *koku* in either of the two successive listings. Thus the sample is restricted to medium and large (but not the largest) holdings. We obtained a total of 175 cases, here considered as discrete, ranging fairly evenly through our 1717–1830 period. Of these 175 cases, between the two successive observations 43 increased by 10 percent or more; 57 were relatively stable, neither increasing nor decreasing by 10 percent; and 75 decreased by 10 percent or more. The rates of exits and entries per 1,000 family-years are calculated in the usual way, with exits (or entries) from the family between the two holding-size observations being multiplied by 1,000 and then being divided by the number of family-years of observation.

16. To control for possible differences in family size (i.e. number of persons at risk per family) between the three groups of families, we converted the rates into number of exits per 1,000 person-years, which then became 36, 43, and 50 for all exits and 13, 23, and 30 for voluntary exits respectively. The χ^2 test was then used to test the null hypothesis that the exit rate was independent of changes in *kokudaka*, assuming that the true exit rate equaled the observed exit rate of the entire sample, and that the expected number of person-years in each family group equaled the observed frequency. For all exits we got a χ^2 of 8.1, significant at the 0.02 level on two degrees of freedom; for voluntary exits we got a χ^2 of 18.5, significant at the 0.0001 level.

17. Five demising families are not represented in this table. (1) One family in which the founder of a branch family returned to the main family after three years is not included in any of our calculations concerning family demise. (2) One "family," consisting of a man and his elder sister both of whom worked as servants outside the village throughout the time they are registered as a household, is not included in demise calculations because it seemed to lack an essential family identity. In any case, its holding size at last observation was 1.8 *koku*. (3) One branch family died out six years after being founded, before its holding size could be recorded in any of our land registers. (4) Two families are missing from the last land listing prior to their demise.

Chapter 8

1. See Smith, "Ōkura Nagatsune and the Technologists."

2. We did not count temporary departures, but only exits (other than death) that proved to be permanent or were intended to be permanent. Included were exits for adoption into another family, moving out of the village, founding a branch family, or any other reason that caused a person's name to be removed from the register listing for his family. In cases where such an exit proved to be temporary (most commonly, where an adoption agreement was nullified and the formerly adopted member returned home), the son's return to his family (and any subsequent departure) was ignored for the purposes of this exercise, and he was not included among the population at risk after his return. In effect, the only exits considered as temporary from the start were those for work as a servant in another household (*hōkō*) in cases (by far the most frequent) where the son returned home at a later date.

3. The total number of female marriages out of families in Nakahara during our period was 184; the total number of person-years for unmarried females aged 15–45 was 2,788.5. Subtracting from these figures the number of marriages and person-years of the daughters who married dur-

ing the years −5 through +5, we subtracted 40 marriages and 215 person-years (which yield the marriage rate of 186). This gave 144 marriages and 2,571.5 person-years for unmarried females 15–45 in Nakahara from 1717 to 1830, exclusive of those in our ten-year sample, yielding a marriage rate of 56.0.

4. Marriage rates in Figure 8.4 were calculated in the same manner as brothers' departure rate (see note 2), except that here only exits for marriage were considered, including second marriages. Marriages before age 15 were not included except in calculating the marriage rate from −5 through +5. The five marriages at younger than age 15 during that period were included because the total of 184 marriages for the entire village in 1717–1830 also included marriages at younger than age 15.

Chapter 9

1. Fruin, *Labor Migration*, pp. 160–61.
2. Hayami, "Tokugawa kōki jinkō hendō no chiikiteki tokusei," p. 76; sex ratios from Sekiyama, *Jinkō kōzō*, p. 270.

Bibliography

Besides the books and articles listed, the following documentary records were used extensively (see Chapter 2). All are deposited in the Meiji hakubutsukan (Records Museum) of Meiji University. We wish to thank Mr. Kanzaki and Miss Kukida of that institution for their help in facilitating the use of this material.

Gonengu narabi sho osameage mono menwari chō, 1716, 1727, 1738, 1746, 1764, 1780, 1792, 1802, 1812, 1823.

Nakahara mura sho hōkōninchō, 1718–1828.

Nakahara mura shūmon oaratamecho, 1717–1830.

Nakahara mura zōnin genin oaratamechō, 1721–1801.

Akimoto Motoya. "Kinsei nōmin kazoku no kibō to keitai," *Mita gakkai zasshi* LXVI, 7 (1973): 65–84.

———. "Kinsei nōmin no kōdō kansatsu," *Mita gakkai zasshi* LXVI, 8 (1973): 64–76.

Aoki Kōji. *Hyakushō ikki no nenjiteki kenkyū*. Tokyo, 1966.

Bergues, Hélène *et al*. *La Prévention des naissances dans la famille*. Paris, 1960.

Blayo, Y., and L. Henry. "Données démographiques sur la Bretagne et l'Anjou de 1740 à 1829," *Annales de démographie historique* (1967), pp. 259–70.

Chandrasekhar, S., ed. *Asia's Population Problems*. New York, 1947.

Charbonneau, H. *Tourouvre-au-Perche au XVIIIe siècle*. Paris, 1956.

Chaunu, Pierre. *Histoire science sociale: La Durée, l'espace et l'homme à l'époque moderne*. Paris, 1974.

Chiang, C. L. *Introduction to Stochastic Processes in Biostatistics*. New York, 1968.

Clark, Colin. *Population Growth and Land Use*. New York, 1967.

Drake, Michael. *Population and Society in Norway*. London, 1969.

Frisch, Rose E. "Demographic Implications of Biological Determinants of Female Fecundity," *Research Paper 6* (July 1974), Center for Population Studies, Harvard.

Fruin, Mark. *Labor Migration in Nineteenth-Century Japan: A Study Based on Echizen Han.* Unpubl. dissertation, Stanford, 1973.

Furushima Toshio. "Shōhin ryūtsū no hatten to ryōshu keizai," *Iwanami kōza Nihon rekishi* XII. Tokyo, 1973: 53–92.

Ganiage, Jean. *Trois villages d'Ile-de-France au XVIIIᵉ siècle.* Paris, 1963.

Gautier, Étienne, and Louis Henry. *La Population de Crulai, paroisse normande: Etude historique.* Paris, 1958.

Gille, H. "The Demographic History of the Northern Countries in the Eighteenth Century," *Population Studies* III, 1 (June 1949): 3–20.

Goubert, Pierre. "Legitimate Fecundity and Infant Mortality in France During the 18th Century: A Comparison," *Daedalus* XCVII (1968): 593–603.

Hajnal, J. "European Marriage Patterns in Perspective," in D. V. Glass and D. C. Eversley, eds., *Population in History* (London 1965), pp. 101–47.

Hanley, Susan B. "Fertility, Mortality, and Life Expectancy in Premodern Japan," *Population Studies* XXXVIII, 1 (Mar. 1974): 127–41.

———— "Population Trends and Economic Development: The Case of Bizen Province," *Daedalus* XCVII (1968): 622–36.

Hanley, Susan B., and Kozo Yamamura. "A Quiet Transformation in Tokugawa Economic History," *Journal of Asian Studies* XXX, 2 (Feb. 1971): 373–84.

———— "Population Trends and Economic Growth in Preindustrial Japan," in D. V. Glass and Roger Revelle, eds., *Population and Social Change* (London, 1972), pp. 451–99.

Hayami Akira. "The Demographic Analysis of a Village in Tokugawa Japan: Kando-shinden of Owari Province, 1778–1871," *Keio Economic Studies* V (1968): 50–88.

———— "Jinkō gakuteki shihyō ni okeru kaisōkan no kakusa," *in* Tokugawa rinseishi kenkyūsho, ed., *Kenkyū kiyō* (1973), pp. 178–93.

———— *Kinsei nōson no rekishi jinkō gakuteki kenkyū.* Tokyo, 1973.

———— "The Population at the Beginning of the Tokugawa Period," *Keio Economic Studies* IV (1966–67): 1–28.

———— "Tokugawa kōki jinkō hendō no chiikiteki tokusei," *Mita gakkai zasshi* LXIV, 8 (1971): 67–80.

———— "Tokugawa kōki Owari ichi nōson no jinkō tōkei," *Mita gakkai zasshi* LIX, 1 (1966): 58–77.

Henry, Louis. *Manuel de démographie historique.* Geneva, 1970.

———— "Fécondité des mariages dans le quart sud-ouest de la France," *Annales* XXVII, 4–5 (1972): 612–40; 977–1025.

———— "Some Data on Natural Fertility," *Eugenics Quarterly* VIII (1961): 80–98.

Hoashi Banri. "Tosenpuron," *in* Takimoto Sei'ichi, ed., *Nihon keizai teiten* XXXVIII (1938): 218–41.

Horie Eiichi. *Meiji ishin no shakai kōzō.* Tokyo, 1954.

Inosaki Tadaichi, ed. *Sansō kōten shūsei.* Ueda, 1927.

Katō Takeo. "Hansei ni okeru Owari no jinkō no bunpu to hendō," *Chiri-gaku hyōron* XXVI, 5 (May 1953): 179–87.

Kellum, Barbara A. "Infanticide in England in the Later Middle Ages," *History of Childhood Quarterly* I, 3 (1974): 367–88.

Knodel, J. "Two-and-a-Half Centuries of Demographic History in a Bavarian Village," *Population Studies* XXIV, 3 (1970): 353–76.

Krause, J. T. "Some Neglected Factors in the English Industrial Revolution," *in* Michael Drake, ed., *Population in Industrialization* (London, 1969), pp. 103–18.

Kumar, Joginder. "A Comparison between Current Indian Fertility and Late Nineteenth-Century Swedish and Finnish Fertility," *Population Studies* XXV, 1 (July 1971): 265–80.

Kuznets, S. "Underdeveloped Countries and the Preindustrial Phase of Advanced Countries," *in* A. N. Agarwala and S. P. Singh, eds., *The Economics of Underdevelopment.* New York, 1963.

Lachiver, M. *La Population de Meulan du XVIIᵉ au XIXᵉ siècle.* Paris, 1969.

Langer, W. L. "Infanticide: A Historical Survey," *History of Childhood Quarterly* I, 3 (1974): 353–65.

Mitsui bunko, ed. *Kinsei kōki ni okeru shuyō bukka no dōtai.* Tokyo, 1952.

Miyakawa Mitsuru, "Ie oyobi kazoku no shiteki tenkai," *Seikatsu bungaku kenkyū* VIII (Dec. 1959): 51–64.

Musumi Takehachi, "Zayū tekagami," *in* Ono Takeo, ed., *Kinsei chihō keizai shiryō* II (Tokyo, 1932), 283–97.

Nakamura Satoru. "Hōken-teki tochi shoyū kaitai no chiiki-teki tokushitsu," *Jimbun gakuhō*, 1964, pp. 130–52.

Nomura kenkyūkai, ed. "Ōgaki hanryō Mino no kuni Motosu gun Kōmi mura no kokō tōkei," *Mita gakkai zasshi* LIII, 10–11 (1960): 166–208.

Nomura Noboru and Yoshii Kitarō, eds. *Kinsei shomin shiryō—Genroku ni okeru ichi shōya no kiroku.* Osaka, 1955.

Ōbata Saizō. "Saizōki," *in* Ono Takeo, ed., *Kinsei chihō keizai shiryō* II (Tokyo, 1932), 399–433.

Ōgaki shi, ed. *Shinshū Ōgaki shishi.* Ōgaki, 1968.

Okuda ke monjo kenkyūkai, ed. *Okuda ke monjo* XI. Osaka, 1974.

Ōkura Nagatsune. "Nōgu benri ron," *Kagaku kōten zenshū* XI (Tokyo, 1963): 75–132.

Perkins, Dwight. *Agricultural Development in China.* Chicago, 1969.

Preston, S. H. "Influence of Cause-of-Death Structure on Age-Patterns of Mortality," *in* T. N. E. Greville, ed., *Symposium on Population Dynamics.* New York, 1972: 201–50.

Sasaki Yōichirō. "Hida no kuni Takayama no jinkō kenkyū," *in* Shakai keizai shi gakkai, ed., *Keizai shi ni okeru jinkō* (Tokyo, 1969), pp. 108–17.

———— "Tokugawa toshi jinkō no kenkyū," *Shikai*, No. 40 (Mar. 1967), pp. 31–44.

Seki Jun'ya. *Hansei kaikaku to Meiji ishin.* Tokyo, 1956.

Sekiyama Naotarō. *Kinsei Nihon no jinkō kōzō.* Tokyo, 1958.

Shakai keizai shi gakkai, ed. *Keizai shi ni okeru jinkō.* Tokyo, 1969.

Smith, Thomas C. *The Agrarian Origins of Modern Japan.* Stanford, 1959.

———— "Farm Family By-Employments in Preindustrial Japan," *Journal of Economic History*, Dec. 1969, pp. 397–423.

———— "The Land Tax in the Tokugawa Period" *in* John Hall and Marius Jansen, eds., *Studies in the Institutional History of Early Modern Japan* (Princeton, 1968), pp. 263–83.

———— "Ōkura Nagatsune and the Technologists," *in* A. Craig and D. Shively, eds., *Personality in Japanese History* (Berkeley, 1970), pp. 127–55.

———— "Urbanization and Premodern Economic Growth: Japan and the West," *Past and Present*, No. 60 (Aug. 1973), pp. 127–61.

Spengler, Joseph. "Demographic Factors and Early Modern Economic Development," *Daedalus*, XCVII (1968): 433–47.

Taeuber, Irene. *The Population of Japan.* Princeton, 1958.

Takahashi Bonsen. *Nihon jinkō-shi no kenkyū.* 3 vols. Tokyo, 1941–62.

Tawney, R. H. *Land and Labour in China.* London, 1932.

Umemura Mataji. "Tokugawa jidai no jinkō sūsei to sono kisei yōin," *Keizai kenkyū* XV, 2 (1965): 134–53.

Utterstrom, G. "An Outline of Some Population Changes in Sweden ca. 1660–1750 and a Discussion of Some Current Issues," in D. V. Glass and D. C. Eversley, eds., *Population in History* (London, 1965), pp. 536–48.

Valmary, P. *Familles paysannes au XVIIIᵉ siècle en Bas-Quercy.* Paris, 1965.

Wigmore, J. H., ed. *Law and Justice in Tokugawa Japan: Materials for the History of Japanese Law and Justice under the Tokugawa Shogunate*, VII. Tokyo, 1972.

Wrigley, E. A. "Family Limitation in Preindustrial England," *Economic History Review* XIX (1966): 82–109.

———— "Mortality in Preindustrial England: The Example of Colyton, Devon, Over Three Centuries," *Daedalus* XCVII (1968): 546–81.

"Yōsan kyōkō roku," *in* Inosaki Tadaichi, ed., *Sansō kōten shūsei* (Ueda, 1927), pp. 397–423.

Index